MADE FOR HEAVEN

A GUIDED LENT JOURNAL FOR PRAYER AND MEDITATION

FR. AGUSTINO TORRES, CFR

ILLUSTRATED BY VALERIE DELGADO

Ave Maria Press AVE Notre Dame, Indiana

Visit our website to find online components, including videos by Fr. Agustino Torres, CFR, to enhance your experience with Made for Heaven *this Lent. Scan the QR code or go to www.avemariapress.com/private/page/made-for-heaven-resources.*

Nihil Obstat: Reverend Monsignor Michael Heintz, PhD
             Censor Librorum
Imprimatur: Most Reverend Kevin C. Rhoades
             Bishop of Fort Wayne–South Bend
Given at: Fort Wayne, Indiana, on 1 August 2023

Founded in 1865, Ave Maria Press is a ministry of the United States Province of Holy Cross.

www.avemariapress.com

Paperback: ISBN-13 978-1-64680-269-2

E-book: ISBN-13 978-1-64680-270-8

Cover and interior images © 2023 Valerie Delgado, paxbeloved.com.

Cover and text design by Brianna Dombo.

Printed and bound in the United States of America.

CONTENTS

INTRODUCTION

We were made for heaven. Even through the traumas, tragedies, and trials, we are created for more. With the eyes of faith, what at first seems like a stumbling block becomes a place where we find God at work, carving out a masterpiece. Still, many of us feel the weight of various situations and we cannot find a way to begin again. Even as you read these words, sorrow, angst, anxiety, and anger choke off the grace that was once yours. "Oh, to return to simpler days," many say. "Would that this or that did not occur," others wonder. Sometimes we wish to run away to a wilderness and hide.

Have you ever been out in the wilderness? As majestic as it may sound at first, the reality quickly begins to sink in that, if we are far from shelter and nourishment, our weaknesses become exposed. In our modern world we have clothed ourselves with distractions, gadgets, and defense mechanisms to shade us from the blinding sun that is our reality. When these begin to melt away, we see how vulnerable we truly are. Our wilderness might be a broken relationship, a lost job, a family tragedy, or just the frustrating fact that memories from our past do not stop hurting.

Jesus went into the wilderness to set our hearts free. The Hebrew people had an understanding of the wilderness as leading to holiness. *Kadesh* is the name of a wilderness in the Bible, and it's related to the Hebrew word *Kadosh*, which means holy. We go through *Kadesh* to become *Kadosh*. Our lives, as they unfold, uncover a constant sequence of potential providence. I say potential because we hold in our hand the latch to a doorway of grace. God has won the victory. Jesus won victory over sin and death by his Cross and Resurrection, but there is something missing from this all-encompassing offering (see Colossians 1:24). What is missing is our offering.

For this we must go into the wilderness. We go into a wilderness not to hide but to become vulnerable enough to admit that we don't have it all together, and that we need to depend on and trust more in Our Lord. Jesus longs to free your heart. God wants your heart to rejoice in freedom. He gives it to you for free, but it came at a great cost. So as to become part of this salvation story, Jesus invites you to journey with him into the wilderness. Not to stay there—but to allow your heart to be captured by joy; for *Kadesh* to become *Kadosh*. God invites us on this journey. His loving mercy will be with you every step of the way. Oh, how good it is to experience his mercy. It will not be easy, but you were not merely made for comfort, you were made for greatness. The joy of Easter can only be understood by those who know a little of its cost. A gift of great worth deserves, in justice, worthy thanksgiving.

Our hearts were created for this. We are invited, therefore, to become who we are! Let us indeed live as we are meant to be, for we are made for heaven. So then, let our hearts journey forth so that Christ may make them free. Unlatch the doorway to the grace that awaits this Lenten season. To truly feel the freedom that flows from the Cross—it is something I deeply desire for all! Full disclosure, it is something I desire for myself, because I am on this journey as well. We were made for heaven. Every one of us.

FR. AGUSTINO TORRES, CFR

HOW TO USE
THIS JOURNAL

The *Made for Heaven* Lent journal's combination of daily meditations, questions for reflection, journaling space, prayers, and beautiful original art is specially designed to draw you into a deeper, richer experience of Lent, preparing you not only to walk with Jesus to Calvary but also to go with him into the desert, to receive his healing mercy, to practice forgiveness, and to meet Jesus in the sacraments of Reconciliation and Holy Communion.

WHO IS MADE FOR HEAVEN FOR?

Made for Heaven is for anyone who desires to dive into the power of prayer, fasting, and poverty to reorient your life toward God. The season of Lent is the ideal time to step back from your life and evaluate where you stand with God, yourself, and others. This challenging journal unpacks different Lenten gospel scenes and New Testament scriptures to help you live what you read while diving deep into the concepts of radical trust, surrender, and prayer.

Made for Heaven is perfect for use in a group setting and was designed with that in mind. There's something special about taking this Lenten journey with a community—whether that community is your entire parish, a small group, or your family. Visit **www.avemariapress.com/private/page/made-for-heaven-resources** for more information about bulk discounts, a leader's guide, help with organizing a small group, videos from Fr. Agustino Torres discussing the theme for each week of Lent, and other resources to help you make the most of your time together with *Made for Heaven*.

You can also use *Made for Heaven* as an individual, with the meditations and journaling prompts helping you draw near to God, hear his voice in new ways, and pour out your heart to him as you turn your attention daily to Jesus's journey to the Cross. You may find that this Lent, you're in special need of regular, quiet times of connection with God. *Made for Heaven* is an excellent way to help you find that space each day.

HOW IS *MADE FOR HEAVEN* ORGANIZED?

Made for Heaven is organized around the idea of returning to the Lord with your whole self with a special emphasis on prayer and poverty:

✦ In Weeks 1 and 2, you set your sights on heaven by taking a vow of poverty for Lent. You'll unpack the ideas of temptation and transfiguration as you enter into the mindsets of Peter, James, and John.

✦ Weeks 3 and 4 challenge you to get outside of yourself and discover how you can give life and living water to others. Your vow of poverty takes an outward turn as you discover how a spirit of detachment frees you to love generously.

✦ In Week 5, you return to the gospel scenes, this time with Martha and Mary. You'll discover how they are models for our prayer and how, through them, Jesus teaches us how to trust him completely.

✦ The final week—Holy Week—calls you to take on Paschal vision and experience the richness of the Church's liturgy, letting it awaken your sacramental imagination. Through deep prayer and rich imagery, you will find yourself immersed in the power of the Cross to conquer death and corruption.

Within each week, you'll encounter a simple daily pattern made up of the following parts:

✦ Each day opens with an *excerpt* from Scripture.

✦ The *meditation* from Fr. Agustino Torres draws out a message from the gospel narrative to help you experience the mercy and love of God this Lent.

✦ The *reflect* section challenges you to ponder and journal in response to the meditation, helping you identify practical ways to live out the Lenten season more fully. The benefits of journaling in this way are enormous—by putting your thoughts, prayers, and resolutions on paper, you take ownership of them in a fuller way, and they, in turn, have greater influence on you.

✦ Finally, after you've read and journaled, the closing *prayer* provides a starting point for your own requests and prayers of thanksgiving and praise to God.

HOW SHOULD I READ MADE FOR HEAVEN?

This Lent journal's daily format is flexible enough to accommodate any reader's preferences: If you're a morning person, you may want to start your day with *Made for Heaven*, completing the entire day's reading, reflection, journaling, and prayer first thing in the morning. Or you may find that you prefer to end your day by using *Made for Heaven* to focus your attention on Christ as you begin to rest from the day's activities. You may even decide to read and pray as a family in the morning and journal individually in the evening.

The key is finding what works for you, ensuring that you have time to read carefully, ponder deeply, write honestly, and connect intimately with the Lord in prayer.

Whatever approach you choose (and whether you decide to experience *Made for Heaven* with a group or on your own), be sure to visit **www.avemariapress.com/private/page/ made-for-heaven-resources** for extra resources to help you get the most out of this special Lenten journey.

Visit **www.avemariapress.com/private/page/made-for-heaven-resources** for more information about bulk discounts, a leader's guide, help with organizing a small group, videos from Fr. Agustino Torres, CFR, discussing the theme for each week of Lent, and other resources to help you make the most of your time together with *Made for Heaven*.

WEEK OF ASH WEDNESDAY

REMEMBER YOUR CALLING

WEEK OF ASH WEDNESDAY

ASH WEDNESDAY

YOU ARE DUST, AND TO DUST
YOU SHALL RETURN.

GENESIS 3:19

YOU ARE MADE FOR HEAVEN

It's Ash Wednesday and everybody is looking for their ashes. It is as if we are beginning a journey into the wilderness. What begins on a Wednesday is to prepare us for a Sunday. What we place on our foreheads is meant to represent what is happening in our hearts—the ashes are meant to open us to new gifts from God. Though some may still be pondering what to do for Lent, we are all invited to fast today. Usually, our fasting should be kept discreet, for the Lord exhorts us not to be obvious about our offering, but to keep it unseen (see Matthew 6:16–18). We often ask one another about our fasting, however, because it's something we're all doing: "How are you fasting? For whom are you fasting? What is the purpose of your sacrifice?" Whatever our personal reasons, our sacrifice is meant to point us to Sunday.

Ash Wednesday is forty-six days before Easter. Perhaps you are thinking that Lent is supposed to be forty days. You would be correct. The reason for the extra days is, quite simply, because Sundays are not counted as part of Lent. When Jesus rose on Sunday, he established Sunday as the prime day for worship. The Jews celebrated the Sabbath (Saturday), but the early Christians called Sunday both the first day and the eighth day because it is the day of Jesus's Resurrection. We were meant for the seventh day of creation—for resting and worshipping God—and ultimately for the *eighth* day, which is an additional day of creation that marks the new life God gives us in the Resurrection. So Sunday points us to our destiny of heaven and eternity. The eighth day is the day that goes beyond seven days into eternity because we are a Resurrection people. This was extremely important for the early Christians. One can even say their lives revolved around being a Resurrection people.

In the early Church, the octagon was a symbol of resurrection. This was reflected in our architecture: some churches were built in the form of an octagon. (Today our stop signs are in the form of an octagon. Perhaps this can be a reminder to us. Every time we see one, we can say, "Stop, I am made for heaven.") For the first Christians and for us, everything points to the Resurrection because it is the event by which we all participate in new life—both here and now, and at the end of time when our bodies are resurrected from the dead (see *CCC* 988).

The question is, where are you going to spend eternity? It is a sobering, but fair, question. Lent is supposed to be a time when we remember who we are and who we are meant to be. We were created to *be* in this world, but were not created *for* this world. We begin this season to internalize this truth more earnestly. Let us begin our journey.

REFLECT

1. Why do you fast? What motivations do you have for the sacrifices or practices you have chosen this Lent?
2. How might you take a moment each Sunday to recall that you are made for heaven?
3. What does the phrase "Resurrection people" mean to you?

_____

_____

_____

_____

_____

_____

_____

PRAY

MY LORD, I AM HERE. SO OFTEN I
FALL, AND I GET DISCOURAGED,
BUT I WANT TO BEGIN AGAIN. HELP
ME BY YOUR GRACE TO STOP AND
REMEMBER THAT I WAS NOT MADE
FOR THIS EARTH, BUT FOR UNION
WITH YOU IN HEAVEN. HELP ME
TO ENTER INTO THIS LENT WITH
RENEWED REPENTANCE AND GREATER
TRUST IN YOUR LOVE AND MERCY.
AMEN.

WEEK OF ASH WEDNESDAY

THURSDAY

AND HE FASTED FORTY DAYS AND
FORTY NIGHTS.

MATTHEW 4:2

SIGNS OF OUR REMEMBRANCE

So, maybe you're ready. You're all fired up to go into your Lenten wilderness and fast, giving up this or doing that. As we embark on this forty-day journey, let us remember the purpose behind our activity. Yes, we take on disciplines so it's easier for us to choose what is good. Ultimately, though, we take on these practices so that we can better respond to God and the new life he gives us.

There's no more fundamental practice for Christians than observing Sunday. It's the day Jesus rose from the dead, so the very first followers marked that day as special. It's the day that we set aside to enjoy the new things God is doing in our lives. So while we focus on prayer, fasting, and almsgiving this Lent, we can't lose sight of what these disciplines are intended to achieve within us. They are ways we can open ourselves more fully to God's love, which broke into our history in a new way in Jesus's Resurrection. So observing Sundays in a special way will keep all of our Lenten efforts grounded in this good news.

Forty days from now, we will enter Jerusalem with Jesus on Palm Sunday. We will enter in a mystical way the place where he shed his blood on the Cross, died, and rose again so that we can come to eternal life. What happened in history on a Sunday is to be lived within each Christian's heart every day.

What does it mean that you are called to be a person of the Resurrection? As you continue your Lenten practices, be sure to observe Sunday as a special day. Share a good meal with your family. Sit down at the table, set aside your phones, and spend time with one another. This is the intent of Sunday, of a holy day: to go to Mass and then to break bread with loved ones. Allow these "extra" days of Lent to become a joyful offering. We have a long journey ahead. Sundays remind us what we are striving for: new life in God.

REFLECT

1. How can you keep in mind that your Lenten practices are meant to open you more fully to God's love and work in your life?
2. In what ways do you wish God to work in your heart this Lent?
3. How might you keep Sunday special as a day to celebrate resurrection joy?

PRAY

THANK YOU, FATHER, FOR GIVING US YOUR SON JESUS AND FOR MAKING US YOUR FAMILY. JESUS, YOU GAVE YOUR LIFE FOR ME, AND ON EASTER YOU ROSE FROM THE DEAD SO THAT I, TOO, COULD RISE WITH YOU. HELP ME TO LIVE IN THE LIGHT OF THE RESURRECTION—TO ENDURE LIFE'S CROSSES AND DIFFICULTIES WITH HOPE IN THE JOY OF ETERNAL LIFE.

WEEK OF ASH WEDNESDAY

FRIDAY

IS NOT THIS THE FAST THAT I
CHOOSE: TO LOOSE THE BONDS
OF WICKEDNESS, TO UNDO THE
THONGS OF THE YOKE, TO LET
THE OPPRESSED GO FREE, AND
TO BREAK EVERY YOKE?

ISAIAH 58:6

IT'S NOT ABOUT YOU

In chapter 9 of Mark's gospel, Jesus and his disciples come upon a ruckus: there's a boy that has a demon. His father says, "If you can do anything . . . ," and Jesus replies, "If you can! All things are possible to him who believes." The man's beautiful reply is, "I believe; help my unbelief!" (Mark 9:22–24). Jesus goes over to the youth and commands the demon to leave, and so it comes to pass. Then his disciples ask, "How come we couldn't do it?" Jesus says that some can only be driven out through prayer and fasting.

Prayer and fasting are among the sharpest tools we have in the spiritual life, and using them together is powerful.

People are discovering the health benefits of fasting. Intermittent fasting, to deprive oneself of certain calories for a certain amount of time, is sometimes healthy. This is wonderful. However, the question arises about the intention of this "fasting." We are invited during this season to allow the Lord to purify the reasons why we do something good. You see, when we fast, we don't fast for ourselves. We don't fast to detox our system and get energy. Those are secondary effects; there's nothing wrong with that. These are good, but they are not the purpose of our fasting. If we're fasting for only ourselves, my brothers and sisters, then we are being invited to go deeper. "Behold, in the day of your fast you seek your own pleasure" (Isaiah 58:3b). As I have heard it said in the Bronx, "It's not about you." This is the fast that God desires: to give food to the hungry, to shelter the homeless. This Friday as we prepare to abstain from meat, let us also offer up something more. Let us not merely check a box. This Lent we are invited to rediscover that our fasting is to enter into deeper relationship—with God and with our brothers and sisters. Lord, help us to go just a little deeper and make things "not just about me." Some things can only be cast out by prayer and fasting.

REFLECT

1. Why is fasting primarily for health benefits missing the meaning of Lent?
2. How might you purify your intentions for fasting?
3. In addition to abstaining from meat today, what is something else you can choose to fast from—a meal, sweets, alcohol, social media?

_____

_____

_____

_____

_____

_____

_____

PRAY

LORD JESUS, YOU FASTED FOR FORTY DAYS. HELP ME TO BREAK AWAY FROM THE THINGS THAT KEEP MY EYES FROM BEING FIXED ON YOU. HELP ME TO HUNGER FOR YOU, OR AT LEAST TO PRAY FOR THAT EVERY TIME I FEEL LIKE BREAKING MY FAST! HELP ME TO OFFER THIS FAST IN SOLIDARITY WITH MY POOR BROTHERS AND SISTERS THROUGHOUT THE WORLD WHO TRULY HUNGER FOR FOOD, AS WELL AS FOR THOSE WHO HUNGER FOR YOU.

WEEK OF ASH WEDNESDAY

SATURDAY

MAN SHALL NOT LIVE BY BREAD
ALONE, BUT BY EVERY WORD
THAT PROCEEDS FROM THE
MOUTH OF GOD.

MATTHEW 4:4

THE FRANCISCAN OPTION—
POVERTY AND SIMPLICITY

As a Franciscan friar, I profess a vow of poverty, and in doing so, I vow to always strive to imitate Jesus who, himself, was poor. This is poverty in a positive sense (dependence on God) and not the poverty that we should all be working to eradicate (destitution and starvation). The idea is that when we imitate Christ in our poverty, we are more interiorly ordered and not governed by material things. Just as prayer and fasting are powerful tools in the spiritual life, so too can poverty help us orient our lives toward heaven. That's because poverty literally makes us poor in spirit: we lack the ability to spiritually feed ourselves and must depend on God's grace and providence. A vow of poverty—spiritual or material—reminds us of this dependence in a concrete way.

Poverty takes many forms—it's really the interior disposition that is most important. The essence of poverty is detachment from anything that is not God. It doesn't mean we starve ourselves or sleep on a rock—it just means that we receive the good things of life with an open hand, delighting in them as gifts but not attaching our desires to them. When we grasp things that are not eternal, they get in the way of our relationship with God.

If you're not a Franciscan, don't worry—you don't need to take on a vow of poverty and wear a simple habit like we do in order to practice simplicity. There are lots of ways we can practice simplicity, and we'll focus on a number of them in the weeks ahead. In fact, every week in the rest of this journal will present a "poverty check" to help you take stock of how you are (or are not) placing your life in God's hands and connecting your life with those who are poor. Each Friday of Lent, we will focus on a particular dimension of poverty and explore how we're able to live it out in the context of our everyday lives.

Poverty is a discipline that we can only take on when we know where we are going; it is a discipline that helps us get to a destination. If we are not focused on where we are going, then we won't have the motivation to discipline ourselves. But if our eyes are set on heaven, then poverty becomes an attractive tool. We gravitate toward it in the same way a football player gravitates to the weight room because he knows that the discipline there will make him better on the field. An Olympic distance runner doesn't enjoy running hills, but she relishes the challenge because she knows it's expanding her lungs and increasing her endurance. Poverty does the same for us—it makes us stronger because it forces us to embrace our weakness and dependence so that we rely solely on God.

I invite you this Lent not only to pray and fast as you've planned but also to take on a practice of poverty in some way. Commit yourself to do away with the ideas, possessions, sins, and even relationships that distract you from heaven.

REFLECT

1. What (or who) has inspired your understanding of the teachings of Jesus's love of the poor and Christ-like poverty?
2. How can you receive what you need to live with a humble and patient spirit of dependence on divine providence?
3. Are you fulfilling Christ's invitation to give to the poor in an ongoing way? Is God asking you to give more to those in need? Do you associate with the poor and enter into a relationship with them?

_____

_____

_____

_____

_____

_____

_____

_____

PRAY

*DRAW ME CLOSER TO YOU, JESUS.
YOU BECAME POOR SO WE COULD
BE ENRICHED. FREE ME FROM
WHATEVER EARTHLY ATTACHMENTS
PREVENT ME FROM LOVING YOU AND
UNDERSTANDING YOUR WILL FOR ME.
GUIDE ME TO SEE THE PRIVILEGE OF
SUFFERING WITH AND FOR THE POOR
AND TO ALWAYS BE GRATEFUL FOR
THE BLESSINGS YOU GIVE ME.*

FIRST WEEK
OF LENT
PRAY THROUGH
THE DESERT

FIRST WEEK OF LENT

SUNDAY

THEN JESUS WAS LED UP BY THE
SPIRIT INTO THE WILDERNESS . . .

MATTHEW 4:1

THE TRIAL OF TEMPTATION

Jesus goes out into the wilderness. We hear in the gospel at Mass today how the Holy Spirit led Jesus into the desert. St. Mark's gospel uses the strong word *drove (ekballei)*. It was the same word used to cast out demons. How is it that the Holy Spirit, who is the Sanctifier, would send Jesus out into the desert in this way?

In a word, it is for mercy. Those who have gone through a period of desolation and have grown spiritually from it know exactly what this means. If pain is not transformed, it is transmitted. Take the time to read the entire gospel for today. There will be a time when the Holy Spirit ushers us into a desert as well, if it has not already happened. After the fact, it may be easy to say that it is a spiritually fruitful time, but this is not the case when one is enduring it. Some people would like others to know when they are in a desert. Others pray earnestly that their time of desolation quickly ceases. Their prayer is "God, help me please! Take me out of here!" Sometimes they ask, "What did I do wrong?" But many times, it is the Holy Spirit who is leading us to this challenge, and the Holy Spirit will lead us through this difficulty. If one does not go through the desert, one would learn to only depend on oneself. Our hearts grow in love when we learn to depend solely on the Lord. The Holy Spirit is leading us into a desert for that change to occur.

Jesus entered the desert to heal the wound caused from the first sin. In Genesis 3:6, the temptations in the garden came in three. They saw that the forbidden fruit was (1) good for food, (2) pleasing to the eye, and (3) desirable for gaining wisdom. St. John summarizes these temptations as the *lust of the flesh* (bodily desire), the *lust of the eyes* (greed), and the *pride of life* (pride, or putting ourselves in the place of God). The triumph of Jesus over his three temptations in the desert brings mercy to us. He endured the trial of temptation, so he is able to forgive us who fall into temptation.

As these temptations reoccur in our own histories, we are given the remedy of fasting, prayer, and almsgiving. The Holy Spirit is moving. Although you may not always see the purpose of your trial, allow the Holy Spirit to move in your desert as well.

REFLECT

1. When you feel as if you are entering a spiritual desert, a time of dryness, how do you usually react?
2. In what ways is the Holy Spirit leading you to change?
3. Are you comfortable with silence? What about silence frightens you?

_____

_____

_____

_____

_____

_____

_____

PRAY

*COME, HOLY SPIRIT! COME AT THE
BEGINNING OF MY LENT AND LEAD
ME TO JESUS. LET JESUS LIVE IN
ME. LEAD ME THROUGH THE DESERT.
QUIET MY MIND AND MY HEART SO
THAT I CAN HEAR THE SOFT WHISPERS
OF YOUR SILENCE AND REST WITH
YOU. I SURRENDER TO ALL THAT YOU
WISH TO DO IN AND THROUGH ME
THIS LENT, BUT BE GENTLE,
GOOD LORD!*

FIRST WEEK OF LENT

MONDAY

HE FASTED FORTY DAYS AND
FORTY NIGHTS, AND AFTERWARD
HE WAS HUNGRY.

MATTHEW 4:2

JESUS HUNGERS
FOR YOUR LOVE

Jesus went into the desert before his public ministry to prepare himself spiritually by fasting. "He was hungry," scripture says, but for what? Have you ever asked yourself what Jesus was hungry for?

As Franciscans, we always receive food by donations, and that comes through building relationships. I was once assigned to a recently established friary, and, at the time, nobody knew us in the neighborhood. We were reduced to eating only peanut butter for a few days. We had made a commitment to begging for food from the people we served, and it was slow going.

I remember saying at the time, "Brothers, we need to pray! I know the Lord is going to do the work." Later that evening I went to celebrate a Mass at a local parish. As I walked into the church a lady approached me with a bag and said, "Father, I don't know why, but I felt like I should go buy you some eggs." I replied with joy, "What? That's awesome! We are so grateful!"

When I returned from Mass the brothers were gathered in a room. As I entered, I hoisted the plastic bag as one holds a treasure and I proclaimed, "Brothers, look! Eggs!" With one voice the brothers shouted out with glee! One would think these eggs were made of pure gold the way we rejoiced at their arrival. We were so happy to have a dozen eggs, because we knew that it was God who provided them. It was a beautiful experience of God's providence. We knew it was from God because we had experienced the lack.

Jesus was tempted in the desert. He was fasting for forty days and forty nights, and his first temptation was to fulfill a legitimate bodily need through illegitimate means. This came right after Jesus was baptized in the Jordan. The heavens opened, and there was a manifestation of God that left all in wonder. Jesus went from this to being alone fasting in the desert for forty days, and he was hungry.

For what did he hunger? Yes, Jesus is truly God and truly man and needed to nourish his body, but really, he was hungry for souls. Think about it: Jesus had in his heart the love for every single human being that had existed or would exist. He has an infinite love for you. He hungers for you to know his love. Yes, this is real, his hunger. His providence often shows us exactly this: Jesus is hungry for your love.

REFLECT

1. What do you feel when you are physically hungry? How does this relate to your spiritual life?
2. What are the spiritual thirsts of your heart? What do you ache for?
3. Do you hunger for souls to know Jesus? Do you notice the hunger of the poor?

_____

_____

_____

_____

_____

_____

_____

_____

PRAY

LORD JESUS, YOU FASTED FOR FORTY DAYS AND FORTY NIGHTS, AND YOUR HUNGER WAS FOR ME TO KNOW YOUR LOVE. HELP ME TO QUENCH YOUR THIRST AND SATISFY YOUR HUNGER BY RECEIVING YOUR LOVE AND LOVING YOU IN RETURN. HELP ME TO HUNGER AND THIRST FOR RIGHTEOUSNESS, TO BRING MANY SOULS TO SATIATE YOUR DESIRE FOR SOULS.

27

FIRST WEEK OF LENT

TUESDAY

THE TEMPTER CAME AND SAID
TO HIM, "IF YOU ARE THE SON
OF GOD, COMMAND THESE
STONES TO BECOME LOAVES OF
BREAD."

MATTHEW 4:3

THE FATHER'S PROMISE

Your identity is in the Father's love for you. The storms of life will send wave after wave to break on this truth, yet this is solid rock.

Your identity is imparted to you by the Father. We often allow other things or forces to define us, but your relationship with God defines you, and his love for you is unbreakable. You are a son or daughter of God, and it is God the Father who is reaching out to you—that is your true identity. Sometimes we feel as if we're different people depending on circumstances. Whatever those influences, they do not define us, nor does our past define us. We are not defined by our failures—we are defined by our identity in God.

Notice how the enemy approaches here; when he's tempting Jesus, he says, "If you are the Son of God . . . " He starts out by questioning the identity of Jesus. Remember, when Jesus was baptized at the Jordan, the voice of the Father said, "This is my beloved Son" (Matthew 3:17). So, this is how the devil starts out, with a quick jab, because he knows that Jesus's mission of salvation is to make God's love known. Jesus wants his identity to be known as the Son of God, as the Savior of the world, as God who is love. So the devil starts attacking him right there because he knows that identity is central to Jesus's mission.

Then he tempts Jesus by saying, "Why don't you turn that rock into bread?" Clever to begin to tempt with something good. That's many times how things start, but Jesus didn't come to do a magic show. All his miracles, all his healings were connected to his mission; they validated his preaching. Sometimes in our relationships, families, or ministries, we take things on to kind of "prove something," maybe even to ourselves. Brothers and sisters, the root of that impulse may be pride. Our task is to allow our actions to be about the mission of salvation.

We might have mixed motives in our actions—do not be alarmed at this. Whatever our motives are, place them before the saving mission of Jesus Christ. Temptations will come. Don't be surprised, but stay close to your identity in Christ and your part in serving in his mission of salvation.

REFLECT

1. What are some failures or weaknesses by which you are tempted to identify yourself?
2. What are some successes by which you are tempted to identify yourself?
3. Imagine your parents were celebrities. How would you feel? How can you more firmly root your identity in being a son or daughter of God?

_____

_____

_____

_____

_____

PRAY

*MY LORD, YOU ARE A KING, AND I
AM YOUR CHILD. YOU ARE A GOOD
FATHER, AND I WANT TO LISTEN TO
YOUR VOICE OF LOVE AND NOT TO
THE VOICE OF TEMPTATION AND
DOUBT. HELP ME TO LISTEN TO YOU.
HELP ME TO KNOW MY DIGNITY AS
BELONGING TO YOU, BEING MADE IN
YOUR IMAGE AND LIKENESS. LET ME
NEVER SEEK MY OWN INTERESTS OR
FEEL THE NEED TO "PROVE MYSELF"
OR EARN YOUR LOVE, BUT LIKE A
CHILD, TO SIMPLY TRUST IN YOUR
GOODNESS AND PROVIDENCE. AMEN.*

FIRST WEEK OF LENT

WEDNESDAY

HE ANSWERED, "IT IS WRITTEN,
'MAN SHALL NOT LIVE BY BREAD
ALONE, BUT BY EVERY WORD
THAT PROCEEDS FROM THE
MOUTH OF GOD.'"

MATTHEW 4:4

GIVE IT ALL TO GOD

Even though Jesus is God, he relies on scripture to respond to the devil's temptation, saying, "It is written, 'Man shall not live by bread alone, but by every word that proceeds from the mouth of God.'" If Jesus uses scripture to fight temptation, maybe we should too! Notice the lesson in his response: it is not just that we shouldn't be concerned about material things, but that we *should* be concerned about spiritual things.

We can also see that the enemy comes at Jesus with a truth. To eat is something that we need for life. He knew Jesus was hungry, and so he said, "If you are the Son of God, why don't you change those rocks into bread?" (see Matthew 4:3). The enemy is constantly trying to invite us to manipulate nature for selfish gain. But Jesus always works miracles to point to his mission of salvation. For example, when the Israelites were going through the desert, God didn't change sand into bread; instead, he caused bread to rain down from heaven in the form of a starchy crust. He didn't change nature; he worked *through* nature. In the same way, in the feeding of the five thousand, Jesus didn't materialize food for the crowd; he took the bread and fish that were already present and multiplied them.

We are learning something about the way Jesus is coming to save us. He didn't come down and say, "You guys really messed this up. I need to change all this because of sin." No, he took on our nature, becoming one of us in all things except for sin. As St. Athanasius said, "He became what we are that we might become what he is." Through our nature he elevated our dignity; through his Death and Resurrection he opened the doors for our human nature to enter into heaven. He fulfilled what is in our nature.

If you look at yourself and say, "My nature isn't good. It needs to change so that I can be better, so that I can be at peace," I implore you, give that thought over to our Lord and let him transform you. I know it's incredibly difficult. But Jesus works through us because he created us as good.

REFLECT

1. Identify a part of you that you don't like, and surrender it to Jesus. Ask God to help you to see yourself through his eyes.
2. In what ways are you overly concerned about material things?
3. How might you focus more on your spiritual needs this Lent? Can you ask Jesus to transform your heart to be more like his own?

_____

_____

_____

_____

_____

_____

_____

_____

_____

_____

_____

PRAY

MY LORD AND MY GOD, HELP ME TO SEE MYSELF AS YOU SEE ME. HELP ME NOT TO LIVE IN THE GAZE OF OTHERS OR OF MY OWN PERCEPTION OF MYSELF, BUT AS A CHILD IN YOUR GAZE. HELP ME TO RECEIVE YOUR LOVE AND ALLOW THAT LOVE TO TRANSFORM ME.

FIRST WEEK OF LENT

THURSDAY

THEN THE DEVIL TOOK HIM TO THE HOLY CITY, AND SET HIM ON THE PINNACLE OF THE TEMPLE, AND SAID TO HIM, "IF YOU ARE THE SON OF GOD, THROW YOURSELF DOWN; FOR IT IS WRITTEN, 'HE WILL GIVE HIS ANGELS CHARGE OF YOU,' AND 'ON THEIR HANDS THEY WILL BEAR YOU UP, LEST YOU STRIKE YOUR FOOT AGAINST A STONE.'"

MATTHEW 4:5-6

MAKE YOUR LIFE
ABOUT CHRIST

Now the enemy comes to Jesus and quotes scripture too. What? The devil knows scripture?

He took Jesus to the Holy City of Jerusalem, to the pinnacle of the temple where the teachers would sit. Picture them there on a terrace on the roof. He said, "Throw yourself down from here, for scripture says the angels will bear you up and you will not cast your foot against the stone." The devil was quoting scripture to God, but it was actually a temptation to pride and ambition. See, Jesus, the Messiah, came to bring the revelation of God's love in his salvation, to fulfill all of scripture.

The pinnacle of the temple is where the teachers of the law would sit and teach. It would be like saying, "I'm gonna make you a professor at Harvard, and from that platform, man, you're gonna be able to reach a lot of people!" Or "Hey, I'm gonna make you a star! You've got talent, and from this platform you'll be able to influence a lot of people. How many followers do you have? You have the makings of an influencer, just sign here, click here, pay this, and I will help you get all the followers that you have ever wanted."

In just this way, the enemy came and said, "Hey, Jesus, you want your people to accept you, right? Throw yourself down, and when the angels lift you up, everyone's gonna say, 'Oh, look! It's Jesus from Nazareth! Yes, I will follow him. I will follow him just like these false teachers." Jesus saw through the temptation and responded, "No."

Today, I want to invite us to pray against those temptations to pride and ambition. We have to make our lives about Christ. If an amazing opportunity comes up, put it into discernment and ask holy people to pray with you and for you so that you can accomplish God's will as he wills it.

REFLECT

1. Have you ever found yourself tempted to fame and honor? How can you look to Jesus to embrace humility?
2. In what ways can you use discernment and prayer to ensure that you pursue new opportunities for God's glory more than for your own?
3. What can you do today to open yourself to being humble, such as praying for humility or serving someone without expecting praise?

PRAY

*JESUS YOU ARE THE KING OF KINGS,
AND YET YOU BECAME A BABY, THE
SON OF A POOR FAMILY, THAT I
MIGHT NOT FEAR TO APPROACH
YOU. HUMBLE ME WITH YOUR
HUMILITY. HELP ME IMITATE YOUR
FAITHFULNESS. NO MATTER WHAT
OPPORTUNITIES ARISE FOR ME, OR
WHAT CHALLENGES I FACE, CENTER
MY HEART ON YOU ALONE. IF I
AM ANCHORED IN YOUR LOVE, NO
STORM CAN TOSS ME. I KNOW I WILL
FIND TRUE HAPPINESS WHEN I FIND
AND DO YOUR WILL.*

FIRST WEEK OF LENT

FRIDAY

HUMBLE YOURSELVES THEREFORE
UNDER THE MIGHTY HAND OF
GOD, THAT IN DUE TIME HE
MAY EXALT YOU. CAST ALL YOUR
ANXIETIES ON HIM, FOR HE
CARES ABOUT YOU.

1 PETER 5:6–7

POVERTY CHECK—
FREEDOM FROM
DISTRACTIONS

Being poor in the things of this world gives us an opportunity to become rich in the things of God. Though God created the world, it is fallen—it does not always reflect God's glory. Power or status or Instagram impressions or money or good grades or beauty or a number on a scale or many other things can all be good as long as they don't become ends unto themselves. Those who are rich in the ways of the world are also rich in distractions. A practice of simplicity and poverty clears away obstacles that impede our ability to hear and respond to the voice of God.

So when you look at your life, what distractions eat up time and attention? It's not that every waking hour has to be trained only on God, but perhaps some of our attachments are preventing us from seeing where God might be breaking into our lives. If our screen-time report tells us we are on our phones for an average of multiple hours each day, what kinds of cues might we be missing out on? How many opportunities to love pass us by because our noses are pointed at a screen? Perhaps our practice of simplicity this week is twofold: first, to become more available by letting go of things that occupy too much of our attention, and second, to be ready to reach out—to God or to a loved one or friend—when we feel the instinct to distract ourselves. Poverty is just the first step; we need to be nimble and ready to respond when opportunities to love present themselves!

Prayer keeps our poverty on track. When we practice poverty, we start to recognize where it "pinches." But then there is freedom, and with freedom, peace and gratitude. Being willing to let things go reveals to us the things that we are holding on to tightly. What do we think we cannot live without? When we practice being poor in spirit, we start to see with clarity what we are clinging to. Usually, what we are clinging to indicates some kind of fear or lack of trust in the Lord. So poverty can help us see where we need the Lord's love to heal us.

Prayer keeps our eyes open to what our poverty is telling us. It also helps us respond with trust when we run into a limitation. When we are confronted with inconvenience or the lack of something we want, we have an opportunity to turn to the Lord.

REFLECT

1. How are you "rich" in the ways of this world? In what ways are you attached to status or power?
2. What do you think you cannot live without?
3. In what ways do you need the Lord's love to heal you?

PRAY

LORD, HELP ME TO TRUST YOU WITH MY WHOLE HEART. SHOW ME WHERE I LACK GENUINE TRUST IN YOU AND HOW I CLING TO THE THINGS OF THIS WORLD. GUIDE ME IN PRACTICING INTENTIONAL DETACHMENT SO THAT I CAN HEAR YOUR VOICE MORE CLEARLY.

FIRST WEEK OF LENT

SATURDAY

AGAIN, THE DEVIL TOOK HIM TO A VERY HIGH MOUNTAIN, AND SHOWED HIM ALL THE KINGDOMS OF THE WORLD AND THE GLORY OF THEM; AND HE SAID TO HIM, "ALL THESE I WILL GIVE YOU, IF YOU WILL FALL DOWN AND WORSHIP ME." THEN JESUS SAID TO HIM, "BEGONE, SATAN! FOR IT IS WRITTEN, 'YOU SHALL WORSHIP THE LORD YOUR GOD AND HIM ONLY SHALL YOU SERVE.'" THEN THE DEVIL LEFT HIM, AND BEHOLD, ANGELS CAME AND MINISTERED TO HIM.

MATTHEW 4:8–11

BEGIN AGAIN

Does the devil own all the kingdoms in the world, or was the Prince of Lies doing what he knows best? This is a very interesting question. Jesus was and is bringing the kingdom of heaven here to us. This is part of God's love to establish his kingdom here on earth. Satan said, "You know what? I'll give you all this. Don't you want everyone to love you? Don't you want all these people whom you love to receive you? I'll give it to you. You want these people? Take them! Just worship me, and it is all yours." Jesus responds by casting Satan out. "No, that's not how you do it," he says. "You never fulfill your purpose at the cost of giving worship to God. This is not a utilitarian endeavor. A moral act is not measured just in the way it turns out. Worship the Lord your God, and serve him only."

My brothers and sisters, Jesus's example shows us that temptation eventually exposes itself. There is an old saying, "The devil always shows his horns." In a time of temptation, we feel as if the battle is raging hard and our strength may be failing, but if we hold on and are patient, the enemy will suddenly flee. "Submit yourselves therefore to God," writes St. James in the New Testament. "Resist the devil and he will flee from you. Draw near to God and he will draw near to you" (James 4:7–8a). What we need to know is that if we hold on, this too shall pass.

Growing up in south Texas, close to the Gulf of Mexico, I would often go to the beach with my family. As a little boy, sometimes the waves would pick me up and sweep me off my feet. There was one time when I was convinced I was drowning. I called out desperately, "Help me, I'm drowning!" Somebody grabbed my hand and said, "Just stand up." What happened is that the wave picked me up, and I got scared, but then it put me back down, but I didn't realize I was standing on solid ground.

This is the same way it is with temptation: it picks you up, and it's a little scary in the moment, but then it lets you down. Temptations do not come to be—they come to pass! We're always given the grace to respond well. After Jesus responds with faithfulness, notice how the devil flees, and then how beautiful angels come and minister to him.

This is an interesting part of this verse because in the Gospel of Luke it says that the devil left him for a time, meaning he was going to come back. The temptation comes, but it's going to come back as long as we're here on earth. Yet, take heart: the angels will continue to minister to us in an ongoing way. We're never alone in our struggles. There's always help.

If you're struggling, say a prayer. In fact, I know there are people who are struggling right now. We just started Lent, and you're already struggling with Lent. You're already thinking, "Oh man, I already messed up. It's been one week. I couldn't get through one week." It's okay. Call on the angels to minister to you, and begin again. And again. And again.

REFLECT

1. Do you feel discouraged as you struggle with your Lenten commitments? If so, how can you approach Jesus in prayer to seek peace, encouragement, and strength to persevere?
2. In what ways can you strive to keep worship of God as a priority in your life among other righteous acts?
3. When you feel tempted, do you turn to God in prayer? Do you experience the comfort of God's grace and his angels when you resist a temptation?

PRAY

LORD, I AM SO TEMPTED TO DISCOURAGEMENT. IT'S ALWAYS ONE STEP FORWARD AND TWO STEPS BACK. I FEEL AS IF I'M DROWNING SOMETIMES. HELP ME TO KEEP MY EYES ON YOU AND NOT ON THE WAVES THAT ARE CRASHING ALL AROUND ME. YOU ARE ENOUGH. YOU WILL MAKE ME HOLY. I CAN'T DO IT, BUT YOU CAN. YOU SAY, "ASK AND YOU WILL RECEIVE." BEHOLD, I AM ASKING, AND, JESUS, I TRUST IN YOU.

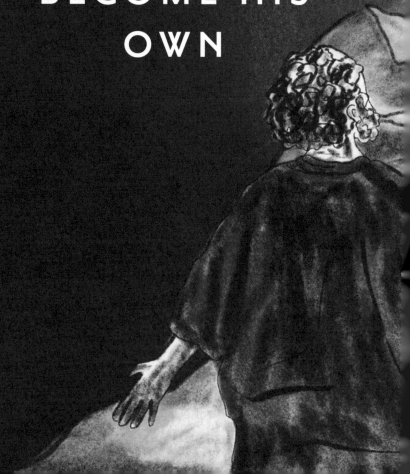

SECOND WEEK
OF LENT

BECOME HIS OWN

SECOND WEEK OF LENT

SUNDAY

AFTER SIX DAYS JESUS TOOK
WITH HIM PETER AND JAMES
AND JOHN HIS BROTHER, AND
LED THEM UP A HIGH MOUNTAIN
APART.

MATTHEW 17:1

BE TRANSFIGURED

Peter, James, and John were invited up the mountain, and there Jesus was transfigured before them, his clothing becoming dazzling white. The Gospel of Luke relates that it occurred while Jesus was in prayer. My brothers and sisters, this is an insight into who Jesus is and how prayer can transform us. The Transfiguration is not a one-hit wonder. It is an outward showing of an internal reality. It is showing who Jesus really is. He is the fullness of revelation; he is God and the Messiah. Jesus is glorious from all eternity, and he allowed his disciples to see it in this moment. It is almost as if Jesus was showing the disciples his inner life. All this for a very good reason. "Show me your glory," Moses said when he went up another mountain and beheld the magnificence of God. He was transformed by this encounter. We are transformed as well when we behold God in prayer.

The Transfiguration is something that happened in the past but is ongoing—it reveals who Jesus is. This event shows us a little bit about his divine nature: the fact that Jesus is the Second Person of the Most Holy Trinity. He was always in union with the Father, always in union with the Holy Spirit, and the Transfiguration is just showing us in time and in history what that looks like.

We, too, are called to be transfigured. As St. John Chrysostom said, "He was transfigured before his disciples, thereby revealing to them the glory of the future things and, as in an enigmatic and dim way, showing what our bodies will be like." Our bodies are meant to imitate Jesus even in this way. Our hearts were created for union with God, and when we draw closer, they become dazzling white. I invite you to ask how God wants to be transfigured in you. This is the thing God wants to do in you. He became man so that we can be divinized, so that we can be one with him in heaven. Pray, hope, don't worry, and let the process start today.

REFLECT

1. Do you wish you could have seen Jesus transfigured? How might you open yourself to seeing Jesus in glory through the sacraments?

2. What do you think of St. Athanasius's words? What do they reveal about God's love for you?

3. Is there something within you that needs to be brought into the presence of God, to be transformed so that you may be able to shine?

PRAY

*LORD, LET ME SEE YOUR FACE.
YOU ARE SO GOOD. WHEN I FOCUS
ON MYSELF, I LOSE HOPE OF EVER
REFLECTING YOUR GLORY. HELP
ME TO LOOK AT YOU, TO INVITE
YOU MORE DEEPLY INTO MY HEART,
SO THAT YOU MAY ENTER IN AND
TRANSFORM ME. SHINE IN AND
THROUGH ME, LORD, SO THAT WE
MAY BE ONE AND MAY DRAW OTHERS
TO YOU.*

SECOND WEEK OF LENT

MONDAY

AND AS HE WAS PRAYING,
THE APPEARANCE OF HIS
COUNTENANCE WAS ALTERED,
AND HIS CLOTHING BECAME
DAZZLING WHITE.

LUKE 9:29

THE LORD
INVITES YOUR HEART

Before ascending the mountain, Jesus had asked the disciples, "Who do men say that the Son of man is?" The disciples came up with some answers: "Oh, I heard some people think you're Elijah, or Jeremiah, or John the Baptist." But then Jesus asked, "But who do you say that I am?" (see Matthew 16:13–15). This question is an invitation to ascend a mountain of self-discovery and arrive at the summit of self-gift so our heart and his may become one. How Jesus must have longed to be truly seen by his friends for such a long time.

And now I ask you: Who do you say Jesus is? Ultimately, we will have to answer this fundamental question. All other things will pass away—*all* other things—and this question will remain. Who do you say Jesus is? To answer this question, Peter, James, and John are drawn away by themselves with the Lord.

Some biblical scholars believe that this happened during the Feast of Booths, which is a Jewish holiday recalling when the Israelites were in the desert. They would camp out, barbecue, and remember, "This is how we had to live when we were out in the desert." It was meant to bring to life the experience in the desert. It was a celebration, and I can imagine that all St. Peter wanted to do was stay and barbecue with his friends. But Jesus said, "Come up with me to that mountain." And Peter must have protested, "Jesus, I just want to barbecue. Can I just stay here? What do you have to do up there? Can't you do it down here? We're barbecuing." But Jesus said to come, and he drew them "apart" (Matthew 17:1). Here it means "by themselves," but the Greek word can also mean "peculiarly one's own."

How the heart of Jesus desires for us to know that he wants us to be peculiarly his, and he ours. This is how love works. My heart is his, and his heart is mine. His precious, loving heart becomes mine. I cannot comprehend the audacity of God that he would entrust such love to me. Yet this is what he does. Jesus drew the disciples to be peculiarly his own.

When Jesus does this to us, we often don't like it. It hurts. We would rather stay where we're at, but God calls us higher. Jesus called Peter, James, and John higher, and one can imagine that they were gasping, wondering why, and wanting to be somewhere else—until they got to the top of the mountain.

REFLECT

1. Where is the Lord asking you to draw away from so that you can be peculiarly his own?
2. How is he inviting you into an experience? One on one? Just you and him?
3. Who do you say Jesus is in your life?

_____

_____

_____

_____

_____

_____

_____

_____

PRAY

*LORD, I WANT TO KNOW YOU. I
WANT TO KNOW WHO YOU ARE AND
NOT JUST MY PERCEPTION OF YOU.
HELP ME TO KNOW YOU. HELP ME TO
CLING TO YOU BOTH IN MOMENTS OF
GLORY AND WHEN I DESCEND DOWN
THE MOUNTAIN. HELP ME TO KNOW
YOUR PERSONAL LOVE FOR ME AND
ALLOW IT TO TRANSFORM ME.*

SECOND WEEK OF LENT

TUESDAY

AND BEHOLD, THERE APPEARED
TO THEM MOSES AND ELI'JAH,
TALKING WITH HIM.

MATTHEW 17:3

YOU BELONG TO GOD

The three disciples saw Moses and Elijah speaking with Jesus. What were they talking about? The Gospel of Luke tells us they were talking about his impending death on the Cross. Jesus had a mission. His entire life was leading to the Cross. His entire existence was meant to bring us salvation. This is why he took on human nature, so that he could save us, but there were those who came before him to prepare the way. All of divine revelation was foretelling this. Jesus said that he didn't come to abolish the Law, but he came to fulfill it. Well, this is what Moses and Elijah represent at the Transfiguration. Moses represents the Law, and Elijah represents the prophets.

Let your heart be drawn to gratitude for those who prepared the way for you. Take a moment and thank God for those who gave you the faith. Through them, God speaks his desire that you be his own.

There is a parallel to the Transfiguration in the story of Exodus when Moses went up the mountain. There, he met with God, who told him to remind the Israelites, "You have seen what I did to the Egyptians, and how I bore you on an eagles' wings and brought you to myself. Now therefore, if you will obey my voice and keep my covenant, you shall be my own possession among all peoples" (Exodus 19:4–5). The Israelites were called to be God's own just like the disciples he called apart in Matthew 17:1 to journey with him up the mountain.

With the Law, we hear rules. Some people do not like rules, because they seem to limit freedom. But we need to understand that the Law was the result of people experiencing liberation and salvation. Moses was given the Law in the context of being freed. Part of the relationship that came from freedom from slavery was a covenant with God. "I will belong to you and you to me," God was saying to his people.

Elijah and the prophets preached to the Israelites who had become unfaithful to this covenant. A prophet is somebody who brings meaning when tragedy strikes, but who also speaks as a voice of God telling us to correct our path—always because of love and mercy.

God longs for his salvation to be more present in your life. His love is waiting for you to become more aware of what needs to die in you so you may fully embrace that love. Just as Jesus was speaking of his coming death at his Transfiguration, we need to put to death the old person we were and begin to walk with Christ in freedom. We see him transfigured here because it's a sign of what we will become in him.

REFLECT

1. What needs to be "put to death" in you so that you may follow Jesus in freedom?
2. How does the Transfiguration inspire you with hope for new life shared with Christ?
3. For whom are you grateful for passing on the faith to you?

PRAY

*THANK YOU, LORD, FOR ALL THE
PEOPLE IN MY LIFE WHO HAVE
PLANTED THE SEEDS OF FAITH
AND HELPED ME TO FOLLOW YOU.
I FEEL YOU CALLING ME HIGHER,
BUT HONESTLY THAT SCARES ME.
I AM AFRAID OF LETTING YOU
INTO CERTAIN PARTS OF MY HEART
BECAUSE I'M AFRAID OF WHAT YOU
WILL FIND THERE AND OF WHAT
YOU WILL ASK OF ME. I RECOGNIZE
THAT THIS IS NOT LOGICAL, THAT
YOU ALREADY KNOW ME FULLY, BUT
MY HEART IS STILL SLOW TO SHOW
YOU THESE PARTS OF ME. PERFECT
LOVE CASTS OUT ALL FEAR. YOU ARE
PERFECT LOVE. PLEASE CAST OUT ALL
FEAR FROM MY HEART.*

SECOND WEEK OF LENT

WEDNESDAY

PETER SAID TO JESUS, "MASTER,
IT IS WELL THAT WE ARE HERE;
LET US MAKE THREE BOOTHS,
ONE FOR YOU AND ONE FOR
MOSES AND ONE FOR ELI'JAH."
FOR HE DID NOT KNOW WHAT
TO SAY, FOR THEY WERE
EXCEEDINGLY AFRAID.

MARK 9:5-6

CONSOLED BY THE CROSS

St. Thomas More was a martyr under King Henry VIII because he famously refused to take an oath that would deny his faith. As chancellor, he was like the vice president of England, but he didn't want to leave the Catholic Church, so he ended up dying a martyr for the faith. Before this, in 1516, St. Thomas More wrote a book called *Utopia,* which is a word we understand today as meaning "a perfect place." We all want to live in paradise. However, St. Thomas titled his book this way to make a point, for *utopia* in Greek means "no place." What this patron of lawyers was trying to teach us is that our dream of creating the perfect world is a longing for heaven.

There's a temptation that we have in the world today, exemplified by Peter's desire to build three tents. We seek to live in consolation, almost saying like Peter, "Let us stay here." Mark's gospel tells us that Peter did not know what he was saying, for he was full of emotion. When we're going through consolation, when everything's going great, we just want to stay there. But at the end of the day, we cannot build our paradise here on earth. Consolations will come to an end; it's part of our struggle here on earth. Anyone can love when it's easy. Jesus is asking us to love even when it's difficult, because otherwise, it's not love.

Pope Benedict XVI in his encyclical *Spe Salvi* said that the modern world sees salvation as a flight from responsibility, a selfish search for salvation, which rejects the idea of serving others. The modern world sees salvation not as faith in Jesus Christ but rather as faith in "progress," which will build our own three tents, our utopia on earth. The fatal flaw of a utopian society is that pleasure or comfort is sought as the predominant value.

My brothers and sisters, I have a question. Is your number one goal comfort? Is your prayer life about wanting to stay in the consolation? We might be faithful to all the practices of

Catholicism, yet still find ourselves saying, "I just don't want to suffer." In many ways this is quite natural, and I have said this myself many times. But we are made for more. It's not about suffering and not suffering. It's about following Jesus, and Jesus goes to the Cross. Everybody wants to be resurrected, but nobody wants to go through Calvary. There's no resurrection without a death. Consolations will come and go. It's Jesus who is the tent or the tabernacle in which we will abide, in whom alone salvation rests.

REFLECT

1. Are you tempted to seek perfect happiness on earth? How does the knowledge that true paradise is only with God give you a new perspective on life?
2. What in Pope Benedict XVI's words inspires you? How is faith and salvation less about comfort here on earth and more about spiritual growth and service of God and others?
3. When you fear suffering and discomfort, how might you ask Jesus for strength to follow him to the Cross?

PRAY

*LORD, THE THOUGHT OF UNCHOSEN
DISCOMFORT MAKES ME VERY
UNCOMFORTABLE. THERE IS A
DESIRE IN ME TO SELECT MY
DISCOMFORT, WHICH IS MUCH MORE
COMFORTABLE. HELP ME TO SEEK
THE GOD OF CONSOLATION AND NOT
THE CONSOLATIONS OF GOD. I HEAR
YOU INVITING ME TO WALK OUT INTO
THE DEEP, BUT I CAN ONLY FOLLOW
IF YOU HOLD ME BY THE HAND. GIVE
ME STRONGER FAITH AND TRUST.
JESUS, I TRUST IN YOU.*

SECOND WEEK OF LENT

THURSDAY

HE WAS STILL SPEAKING, WHEN
BEHOLD, A BRIGHT CLOUD
OVERSHADOWED THEM, AND A
VOICE FROM THE CLOUD SAID,
"THIS IS MY BELOVED SON, WITH
WHOM I AM WELL PLEASED;
LISTEN TO HIM."

MATTHEW 17:5

GOD'S ABIDING PRESENCE

Do you ever have questions about the faith? Why did Jesus have to die? What do we believe about the Virgin Mary? Why do we have relics? Have you ever said to yourself, "I'm Catholic, but I struggle with this"?

Our struggles are not the same thing as despairing of our salvation. To have questions is how we grow in knowledge about something. What lover would not want to ask his beloved questions to know more about her? One thing that you need not question is that God's presence will abide with us forever. Lord, deliver us!

But Jesus kicks it up a notch. Now, in the Old Testament, a lightning cloud signaled the presence of God. In Exodus 33:7–9, Moses put together a tent called the "tent of meeting" where he would converse with God. Then a shiny cloud came over the tent to show that the presence of God was there. In 1 Kings 8:10, this same cloud filled the house of the Lord at the dedication of the Temple; it was called the Shekinah Glory. This Shekinah Glory is the abiding presence of Yahweh over this tent. Now what we are seeing here at the Transfiguration is the Shekinah Glory as it comes over Jesus.

Why? Where's the tent? Well, remember that John 1 says Jesus, the Word of God, "became flesh and dwelt among us" (John 1:14). The actual translation is "he tabernacled among us"; he set his tent up among us. Jesus is the abiding presence; he is in the tabernacle in every single Catholic church. When we see that red candle lit, we can believe and know that his presence is there. We need not be afraid. This is what God the Father was showing us at the Transfiguration.

Notice that God addressed Peter, James, and John: "This is my Son. Listen to him." God wasn't speaking to Jesus. Jesus knows who he is. Those words are addressed to us. We need to grow in faith that Jesus's abiding presence will always be with us.

Oh, how we struggle when we feel God is not near. We doubt God is close to us. We wonder if he is there. We struggle, at times, to see God in the Church because of the weakness of her ministers. Let us trust with every fiber of our being that God is near us in the tabernacle, our own local "tent of meeting." Listen to the Father's voice say, "This is my Son. Listen to him." For he will never leave us.

REFLECT

1. In what ways do you sometimes struggle to recognize that God is near to you?
2. What might help you see and value God's closeness to you through the sacraments, the Church, or the love of others?
3. How might you better appreciate Jesus's true presence in the tabernacle and take time to speak with him there?

_____

_____

_____

_____

_____

_____

PRAY

*LORD, SOMETIMES I FEEL SO ALONE.
I KNOW YOU ARE EVERYWHERE,
BUT I DON'T FEEL YOU. I TURN IN
ON MYSELF AND WONDER IF I DID
SOMETHING WRONG, IF IT'S BECAUSE
I DON'T KNOW HOW TO PRAY
PROPERLY. IN MY ISOLATION AND
LONELINESS, I MAKE IT ALL ABOUT
ME. GIVE ME THE GIFT OF FAITH SO
THAT I MAY CHOOSE TO BELIEVE
THAT YOU ARE CLOSER TO ME THAN
I AM TO MYSELF, THAT YOU ARE
FAITHFUL. YOU SAY YOU WILL NEVER
FORSAKE OR ABANDON ME.
JESUS, I TRUST IN YOU.*

SECOND WEEK OF LENT

FRIDAY

WHEN THE DISCIPLES HEARD
THIS, THEY FELL ON THEIR
FACES, AND WERE FILLED WITH
AWE. BUT JESUS CAME AND
TOUCHED THEM, SAYING, "RISE,
AND HAVE NO FEAR."

MATTHEW 17:6–7

POVERTY CHECK—
FREEDOM FROM FEAR

At hearing the incomprehensible voice of God, the disciples who were invited to the mountaintop fell to the ground in fear. The disciples also heard the voice of God when Jesus was being baptized, but they didn't fall on their faces then. St. John Chrysostom says that because they had now ascended to the heights, not just physically, but also in their awareness of who God is, they responded appropriately. And isn't it true? The more we learn about God, the more we're aware of how great he is and how little we are, how hurtful were our sins and how great his mercy. It is good and at the same time sobering to draw nearer to this God who is love.

The disciples were filled with *fear*, a word that is also translated as "awe" or "reverence." Fear of the Lord is a fruit of the Holy Spirit; it is a deep love for God in which you desire his abiding presence and do not want to do anything that would separate you from him. The fact that God wants to draw us closer should fill us with some sort of holy fear. The fact that when we go to Mass we receive Communion—the body, blood, soul, and divinity of God—in our own bodies should give us some healthy fear, knowing who we are. The Eucharist is pure gift. We are not entitled to it, but Jesus desires to be ours and we his.

Holy fear is good, but many times it is elusive. It seems our world today has a different type of fear. We can be so afraid to get out of our own comfort zone. Maybe we're trapped in the world of fear, a cycle of anxiety. This is why Jesus touched them and said, "Rise, and have no fear." He tells us: "Your sins that you've confessed are forgiven, and the ones that you haven't confessed can be—come to me!"

Check in on your practice of poverty: "deprive" yourself of unholy fear and fill yourself up with surrender. Let the Lord redeem your fear and give you strength. We know we don't have it all together, but he calls us nonetheless to let go of our anxiety and to embrace him as he touches us and says, "Rise, and have no fear."

REFLECT

1. What are your "unholy fears," and how can you turn them over to the Lord?
2. How can you cultivate dependence on the Lord and start to rely more on him for what you need in your interior life?
3. How can you allow God's peace to transform your anxieties, especially as you receive him in Holy Communion?

_____

_____

_____

_____

_____

_____

PRAY

LORD, I AM SURROUNDED BY SO MANY FEARS AND ANXIETIES IN MY LIFE. BUT YOU ARE GREATER THAN THEM ALL. HELP ME NOT TO FEAR ANYTHING EXCEPT LOSING MY RELATIONSHIP WITH YOU. YOU WILL ALWAYS PROVIDE FOR MY EVERY NEED, AND I BEG YOU TO GIVE ME A GRATEFUL HEART AND A SPIRIT OF AWE AND REVERENCE. I SO OFTEN FOCUS ON MY EVERYDAY PROBLEMS INSTEAD OF FOCUSING ON YOU, WHO HAVE ME IN THE PALM OF YOUR HANDS.

SECOND WEEK OF LENT

SATURDAY

AND AS THEY WERE COMING
DOWN THE MOUNTAIN, HE
CHARGED THEM TO TELL NO
ONE WHAT THEY HAD SEEN,
UNTIL THE SON OF MAN SHOULD
HAVE RISEN FROM THE DEAD.

MARK 9:9

SHARING GOD'S GLORY

Jesus commanded the apostles to tell no one about their vision on the mountaintop until the Son of Man be raised from the dead. Perhaps the disciples were challenged by this request. Would not so many more have come to believe in him if they heard what they saw? But Jesus asked them to be silent. Aren't we supposed to share God's glory? The answer is yes, but not always in the timing that we think. God uses the dark times of our lives, the things that we don't understand, and he needs us to be faithful to him when we cannot see the logic of what is being asked.

Deuteronomy 17:6 and Hebrews 10:28 speak of the law requiring that there be three witnesses before the condemnation of a man. So, if a man committed murder and was facing the penalty of death, two or three witnesses were needed to condemn him. Similarly, it's interesting that after the Resurrection, three disciples—John, James, and Peter—would have shared with the others what they had experienced. "Hey, guys, remember when Jesus took us up that mountain? Well, let us tell you what we heard and saw." Maybe they shared this story in the difficult time after the Resurrection, perhaps in those days before the Holy Spirit descended upon them in the upper room, when they were fearful because Jesus had ascended, when their hearts were nervous because he was gone. Imagine the scene: all the disciples in the upper room, so unsure of what to do. And then the three were able to give testimony about what they had seen when Jesus was transfigured. The three of them would have met the legal standard to establish the truth of the event, not for someone's condemnation to death, but in the glorious truth of Jesus's divinity.

We have seen the glory of the Lord. We have seen him act in our lives. I challenge you to bring this gentle reminder, this word of life, to at least one person today. Maybe it is simply in a situation where someone is tempted to complain; listen to them earnestly, then help them to see the bright side and be grateful. Maybe someone is going through an incredible darkness, an incredible tragedy. You can be the voice of Jesus at that time, saying, "I have seen the glory of God work time and time again in my life, and you will see him work in your life as well." Share your story about the dark times that you lived through and how God has shown his faithfulness. Be the reminder of God's glory to those you meet today.

REFLECT

1. Do you ever feel challenged by God's timing? How might you trust God and be reassured of his presence in the midst of difficult times?
2. When have you experienced God's faithfulness?
3. How can you share the truth of God's faithfulness with someone in your life this Lent?

PRAY

*LORD, YOU HAVE BEEN SO GOOD TO
ME. HOW EASILY I CAN FORGET THIS!
YOU COME TO MY RESCUE, AND I'M
SO THANKFUL, BUT THEN THE NEXT
DAY SOMETHING ELSE COMES UP.
I BECOME ANXIOUS AND WORRIED,
AND I FORGET THAT YOU WILL TAKE
CARE OF EVERYTHING. I WANT TO
REMEMBER, AND I WANT TO SHARE
YOUR GOODNESS WITH SO MANY WHO
I KNOW ARE LOSING THEIR HOPE.
GIVE ME THE GRACE AND COURAGE
TO SHARE MY STORY AND BRING
OTHERS TO YOU.*

THIRD WEEK
OF LENT

TURN
TOWARD GOD

THIRD WEEK OF LENT

SUNDAY

SO HE CAME TO A CITY OF
SAMAR'IA, CALLED SY'CHAR,
NEAR THE FIELD THAT JACOB
GAVE TO HIS SON JOSEPH.
JACOB'S WELL WAS THERE, AND
SO JESUS, WEARIED AS HE WAS
WITH HIS JOURNEY, SAT DOWN
BESIDE THE WELL. IT WAS ABOUT
THE SIXTH HOUR.

JOHN 4:5–6

FINDING JESUS AT THE WELL

Having just preached and confronted leaders in the busy city of Jerusalem, Jesus was traveling in Samaria—and he was tired. He sat down wearily beside Jacob's well, at about noon, when the heat of the day was burning down upon a barren land. A woman came at that time to draw water. Why would anyone be going out in the heat of the day? This woman had adjusted her daily schedule to accommodate her desolation. Water was usually drawn during the cooler times of day because it was hard work. In the morning, all the other women would've been there, gossiping about her: "How many husbands does she have?" "Oh, I don't even know. I've lost count." She didn't want to deal with any of that. She adjusted to stay in mediocrity. But Jesus was waiting at the well.

Perhaps we can relate to her, for many of us have a spirit of self-loathing, of self-hatred. No matter how hard we try, we can't change this inner disposition that tells us we're not good enough. It is difficult to receive love. There are some saints who struggled similarly. St. Francis turned his self-loathing into a vehicle for deeper conversion. For him, self-hatred became a gift of self.

Here are three tips to help us understand. Number one: bad self-hatred has pride as its root. This means that it can be all about oneself. Beware, even our Confession can be prideful: Are we more disappointed that *we* sinned or that we offended God? A holy disposition would lead to humility, focusing more on God and his mercy.

Tip number two is that bad self-hatred leads to self-destruction, whereas a holy sense of self leads to a deepening of conversion. Maybe somebody has given us a correction and we're just crushed; we can't go on. We need to deepen our understanding of where that's coming from. If you're the one giving a correction, it should be rooted in joy and love. Parents, it is possible to discipline with joy in your heart when you see your call as a gift.

The third tip is that bad self-hatred is actually a lie, whereas holy self-gift rejoices in the truth. We need to remember our dignity as children of God, that we are loved, not because of what we do, but because of who we are—because of *whose* we are.

So, on this day, recognize that there might be something that needs to change. The fact that you recognize it is the beginning of a conversion. Let it be a holy, deepening conversion and not a destructive form of self-hatred, and you, too, will find Jesus waiting for you at your well.

REFLECT

1. Do you ever feel tempted to stay in mediocrity? In what ways does Jesus call you to conversion and spiritual growth?
2. Do you struggle with feeling not good enough or with self-loathing? How might trust and dependence on God's mercy help you move toward knowing you are loved?
3. How can you share correction with others in a spirit of joy and love?

_____

_____

_____

_____

_____

PRAY

*LORD, IT IS SO EASY TO GET
DOWN ON MYSELF. I WANT TO DO
THINGS RIGHT, BUT SO OFTEN I
SEEM TO MESS EVERYTHING UP. I
GET SO DISCOURAGED. AND THEN
I GET DISCOURAGED THAT I AM
DISCOURAGED! IT'S LIKE A DEEP
PIT THAT I CAN'T GET OUT OF.
REACH DOWN AND SAVE ME. LORD,
DRAW ME OUT OF THIS PIT AND SET
MY FEET ON SOLID GROUND (SEE
PSALM 40:2). YOU CAN BRING GOOD
OUT OF EVERYTHING. TURN MY
FRUSTRATIONS AND FAILURES INTO
SOMETHING THAT WILL GLORIFY YOU.*

THIRD WEEK OF LENT

MONDAY

THERE CAME A WOMAN OF
SAMAR'IA TO DRAW WATER.
JESUS SAID TO HER, "GIVE ME A
DRINK." THE SAMARITAN WOMAN
SAID TO HIM, "HOW IS IT THAT
YOU, A JEW, ASK A DRINK OF ME,
A WOMAN OF SAMAR'IA?" FOR
JEWS HAVE NO DEALINGS WITH
SAMARITANS.

JOHN 4:7, 9

GIVE EACH OTHER DRINK

The Samaritan woman said to him, "How is it that you, a Jew, ask a drink of me?" She corrected Jesus. She reminded him, "Our people don't talk to each other. What are you doing? You do not belong here in my neighborhood."

There's history here. The land of Samaria actually used to be part of the kingdom of Israel, but it got conquered by the Assyrians three hundred years before the birth of Christ, and they started intermarrying. For the Israelites, it was so important to marry within their own people because this was how God's revelation would continue forward. Intermarrying with the Assyrians made the Samaritans a mixed people in the minds of the Jews at the time of Jesus. A Jew wouldn't sit at the same table or even use the same fork as a Samaritan; there was even violence between the two groups.

Samaritans and Jews did not talk to each other. When Jesus said, "Give me water to drink," this Samaritan woman said, "Wait, hold on; there are a whole bunch of reasons why I shouldn't do this."

But with this one request, God would undo centuries of division. This is what Jesus is teaching us with one gesture, with one invitation, with one encounter. We, too, can do the same in the name of Jesus. Divisions exist in our Church. Divisions exist in our society. Divisions exist within our own race, within our own ethnicity. We judge people, and that's not of God. Jesus is challenging us to overcome these barriers and say, "Let us give each other to drink." We have a way to quench the thirst of Christ, who longs for union no matter what the history is, no matter what the battles of the past. Today is a day to come together as a people of God.

REFLECT

1. What divisions do you find within your home or community? How might you ask God to bring unity to these divisions?
2. In what ways might God be calling you to put aside judgment and seek unity with others?
3. Can you be a peacemaker among people you know who are divided in some way?

_____

_____

_____

_____

_____

_____

_____

_____

_____

_____

PRAY

*LORD, THERE IS SO MUCH DIVISION
ALL AROUND ME. SOMETIMES I FEEL
STUCK IN THE MIDDLE. HELP ME
TO BE A PEACEMAKER. GIVE ME THE
WISDOM TO KNOW THAT YOU ARE THE
MESSIAH, NOT I, BUT THAT YOU WILL
BRING ABOUT UNITY AND WILL HELP
ME TO LOVE PEOPLE IF I FOLLOW
YOU. PLEASE BRING PEACE TO MY
FAMILY, MY NEIGHBORHOOD, MY
COUNTRY, AND THE WHOLE WORLD.
BRING PEACE TO MY
OWN HEART.*

THIRD WEEK OF LENT

TUESDAY

JESUS ANSWERED HER, "IF YOU
KNEW THE GIFT OF GOD, AND
WHO IT IS THAT IS SAYING TO
YOU, 'GIVE ME A DRINK,' YOU
WOULD HAVE ASKED HIM AND HE
WOULD HAVE GIVEN YOU LIVING
WATER."

JOHN 4:10

RIVERS OF LIVING WATER

Who was that person who spoke to you about God? What would have happened if somebody hadn't spoken to your heart about God? What would your life be like without God?

The Samaritan woman had seen it all. Sin hardens the heart. When she came to the well, she saw a man, and he asked for a drink. What did her heart, her hardened and damaged heart, think? Perhaps a woman who had many dealings with men thought the worst. And then Jesus said, "If you only knew who it is that is asking you, you would ask him for living water." Jesus came with a divine word, and it began to change her heart. The world needs the hope that God is giving us because it is a hope that we can't seem to find in all the world's inventions and gadgets and distractions.

When on a mission trip in Vienna, a woman approached us while we friars were walking through a park. She was dressed all in white, and I remember her hair was golden blond, and I thought for a second, "Is she an angel?" And so as I kept on walking, looking at the trees, she came to me and asked with her accent, "Excuse me, why are you dressed this way?" In an attempt at humor I said, "Well, we're dressed this way because we're following Jesus. You've heard of Jesus, right?" She looked at me with all seriousness and said, "No, I've heard his name, but I do not know his story." I began to explain in the simplest of terms who Jesus is. "Jesus is the Son of God. He is God but sent now to the world because there was a gap between us and God, and we could not overcome it, only he could. So that's why he came down to save us: because he loves us. And he died for us on the Cross to open the gates for paradise so that we can be with him in heaven."

She soaked in every single word. She asked, "Would Jesus also love me?" "Yes, Jesus loves you!" was my joy-filled response.

"Could you come and talk to my friends? Because they should know about Jesus as well." She brought me back to her friends, and I told the same story—which didn't have the same effect on them as it did with her. But she shined now with an inner joy at learning about Jesus. I encouraged her to connect with a group from church that I had met and to become more active in this faith that spoke to her heart.

God can speak through any one of us. There are people around you who are longing to hear that there are rivers of living water to quench their thirst.

REFLECT

1. Who has shared the faith with you, and how might you express gratitude to them (perhaps through prayer or in a note or phone call)?
2. Is there someone you could share your faith with? How might you be more open to the prompting of the Holy Spirit to share the Good News with others?
3. How does your faith in God change your perspective on life and how you live?

PRAY

*LORD, SOMETIMES I TAKE MY FAITH
FOR GRANTED. I FEEL AS IF I'VE
HEARD THE STORY OF SALVATION SO
MANY TIMES, AND IT JUST DOESN'T
REALLY SINK IN. HELP ME TO REALIZE
HOW MUCH YOU LOVE ME, HOW YOU
GAVE YOUR LIFE FOR ME BECAUSE
YOU WANTED ME TO BE FREE. LET
THIS TRUTH PENETRATE MY HEART SO
THAT IT WELLS UP IN GRATITUDE SO I
MAY JOYFULLY SHARE IT
WITH OTHERS.*

THE WOMAN SAID TO HIM, "SIR,
GIVE ME THIS WATER, THAT I MAY
NOT THIRST, NOR COME HERE
TO DRAW."

JOHN 4:15

JOSEPH'S YES

When someone is wounded, they often respond with defensiveness. That is how I am hearing the response of this woman. She was offered something divine and responded with the sarcasm that often becomes a coping mechanism to deal with deep pain. Jesus loved her through her response. We are seeing a woundedness that she was not even aware of.

In the aftermath of a worldwide pandemic, I think we are still not sure about all that happened to us. Our hearts need healing. Some still feel abandoned by the Church and its leaders. Some have a lingering hurt at not being able to be there with their loved ones at the moment of death. Others feel let down by the powers that be who often said one thing and then did something completely different soon after. This has had a wounding effect on us, and many of us feel defensive.

The Church stands by her people and accompanies them on their journey. St. Joseph is a great example of this unwavering commitment. Despite his quiet demeanor, he played a vital role in the Holy Family's life, always ready to be a strong and reliable presence for Mary and Jesus.

While Mary is often praised for her "yes" to giving birth to Jesus, we should not overlook Joseph's "yes" and his critical contribution to Jesus's upbringing. As Jesus's foster father, Joseph's role was essential in shaping Jesus's human experience. In John 4, Jesus demonstrates incredible patience when speaking with the Samaritan woman. Could Jesus have seen this patience in Joseph, who was so steadfast throughout his life?

During these challenging times, when many things seem upside-down, it's crucial to remember to be grateful for what we have and to be mindful of those who are on the margins. St. Joseph's example teaches us to respond to difficulties with gentle, clear, and firm actions, always grounded in patience and charity. If we find ourselves frustrated with a family member, we should seek St. Joseph's intercession and remember that we all have a mission to fulfill during this time. If a coworker has a way of pushing your buttons, how can you see that person as God sees them? By being prayerful, hardworking, and charitable, we can honor St. Joseph's legacy and make a positive impact on the world around us.

REFLECT

1. Do you feel wounded by recent experiences of suffering such as the global pandemic? How can you accept Jesus's offer of healing grace?
2. How might you respond to difficult situations and people who challenge you with patience and gentleness like Jesus and St. Joseph?
3. What other lessons might Jesus have learned from St. Joseph that you could apply to your own family or personal life?

_____

_____

_____

_____

_____

_____

_____

_____

_____

PRAY

ST. JOSEPH, I ASK FOR YOUR
INTERCESSION. HELP ME TO REMAIN
IN A SPIRIT OF PEACE, UNITED
TO JESUS. HELP ME TO RESPOND
TO DIFFICULT SITUATIONS AND
DIFFICULT PEOPLE WITH A CALM AND
GENTLE STRENGTH THAT IS PATIENT
AND KIND. BE NEAR ME, ST. JOSEPH.
BE A FATHER TO ME AND TEACH ME.

THE WOMAN SAID TO HIM,
"SIR, I PERCEIVE THAT
YOU ARE A PROPHET. OUR
FATHERS WORSHIPED ON THIS
MOUNTAIN; AND YOU SAY
THAT IN JERUSALEM IS THE
PLACE WHERE MEN OUGHT TO
WORSHIP."

JOHN 4:19–20

HEALING OUR DIVISIONS

I had the distinct pleasure of being at an event and conversing with Matt Maher, a well-known Catholic musician. I asked him about a positive interaction someone had with his music. He paused for a second then responded with a story from a few years ago. A man came up to him after a concert and shared that he was at the point of taking his own life in his truck when a song that Matt Maher had written came on the radio. It gave the young man the courage to turn away from the dark thing he was considering and get help. Matt was amazed that a song could have such an effect on someone.

Did you know that your actions can affect people you may not even see? Some may think that their actions have no impact, but our actions have ripples that extend beyond us and even beyond our circles of friends. Those actions can be like a light or a darkness that affects others—they can bring people healing or increased hurt.

In the Bible, Jesus spoke to a Samaritan woman who brought up a division that was evident in their time. People worshiped in different places, creating a worldly division in religion. We still have divisions today, and it's disheartening that we cannot have communion as we should. It is a prayer of many that one day we may be one as Jesus and the Father are one. Division in religion, society, politics, and family hurts, and many people are wounded from it.

We must have a plan to continue worshiping God in spirit and truth. The Holy Spirit can descend upon us wherever we are, and we can call on him to enter our homes and lead us in prayer. We must challenge ourselves to be faithful and ensure that our actions have a positive impact on others, even those we may not see. Tomorrow is a new day, and we can continue on our journey toward holiness.

REFLECT

1. Have you ever been moved or changed by music or by the words of someone who did not know the effect they were having? How have you seen the Holy Spirit work in this way?
2. How can you pray for and work toward unity in your parish or community?
3. In what ways might you help to build people up through your words and actions instead of tearing down, even unintentionally?

_____

_____

_____

_____

_____

_____

PRAY

*LORD, HELP ME THIS DAY TO BE
AWARE OF THE PEOPLE YOU ARE
PLACING IN MY LIFE AND AWARE OF
THE MISSION THAT YOU GIVE ME
EACH DAY. HELP ME TO BRING YOUR
LIGHT. SOMETIMES I AM SO CAUGHT
UP IN MY OWN STUFF THAT I AM NOT
EVEN AWARE THAT I AM SPREADING
FRUSTRATION AND DOUBT OR
PERHAPS JUST INDIFFERENCE. I WANT
TO BRING JOY TO OTHERS. HELP ME
TO RECEIVE YOUR JOY AND TO BE
INTENTIONAL ABOUT BRINGING IT
TO OTHERS, IF ONLY THROUGH A
GENUINE SMILE.*

THIRD WEEK OF LENT

FRIDAY

WHOEVER DRINKS OF THE WATER
THAT I SHALL GIVE HIM WILL
NEVER THIRST; THE WATER THAT
I SHALL GIVE HIM WILL BECOME
IN HIM A SPRING OF WATER
WELLING UP TO ETERNAL LIFE.

JOHN 4:14

POVERTY CHECK—
GETTING OUTSIDE
OF YOURSELF

This woman from Samaria was poor. She was materially poor (she had to walk a great distance to get water; it wasn't flowing from her yard). She was emotionally poor, looking for love in so many broken relationships. She was spiritually poor, but she knew the Messiah was coming. Jesus went out of his way to meet her. Her poverty made her open to receiving everything from Jesus. As we shall see later, her heart was awaiting the Lord.

The poor teach us so much. What a wealth of encounter awaits us when we go out and enter into relationship with those who are hungry, thirsty, or a stranger. Jesus says in Matthew 25:40 that whenever you loved one of these, "you did it to me."

There's a caution here, though: in striving to fulfill the Gospel, many well-intentioned Christians serve the poor more for their own benefit, rather than for love. Many times, we feel good after serving others, and this can become a drug. This shallow reasoning for service to the poor shrivels up, however, in the heat of difficulties and inconveniences. Ultimately, then, the root of our service is self-serving. We all begin here, so do not be too hard on yourself, but we are not called to stay here. The poor do not exist for the sake of your meditation. They are thirsty, and when we give them to drink, we all are satiated.

I don't know where you live, but I know that there are poor people around you. Maybe you're the poor person. Even still, there is something that you can give to get out of yourself. I challenge you to feed the poor. Make an extra sandwich on your way to work, and give it to somebody who is going to be there on the way. Visit some sick person. It might be a little bit complicated, but pray for them, be aware of them, offer some sort of service.

Volunteer at a soup kitchen, or organize something in the church to do some work for the poor or for someone other than yourself.

The friars often take what we call mercy walks. We simply walk and speak to people, especially our brothers and sisters who live on the streets. We treat them like human beings. It might be the first time anyone treated them with any kindness that day. We all thirst for this. Let us help to quench the thirst.

REFLECT

1. What can you learn from those who are poor in some way?
2. Is there a practical way that you can serve the poor in your community this week?
3. How can you purify your intentions for serving the poor so that you do so not to be self-serving but to serve God and others generously?

_____

_____

_____

_____

_____

_____

_____

_____

PRAY

*LORD, HELP ME TO SEE YOU AND
SERVE YOU IN THE POOR. LET ME
NOT USE THE POOR TO FEEL GOOD
ABOUT MYSELF; LET ME LEARN FROM
THEM HOW TO DEPEND UPON YOU
FOR EVERYTHING. LET ME SEE YOU IN
THEM. LORD, IN YOUR MERCY, USE
ME TO LET THEM SEE YOU AND YOUR
LOVE FOR THEM.*

THE WOMAN SAID TO HIM, "I KNOW THAT MESSIAH IS COMING (HE WHO IS CALLED CHRIST); WHEN HE COMES, HE WILL SHOW US ALL THINGS. JESUS SAID TO HER, "I WHO SPEAK TO YOU AM HE."

JOHN 4:25–26

LET JESUS IN

Have you ever had a secret? Not a scandalous one, but just something you wanted to share with someone? Has anyone ever come up to you and asked, "Can I tell you something? Don't tell anyone." Your attention is immediately captured, and you listen. I am not speaking about gossip or detraction, which are sinful and should be worked on as you grow in your conversion.

As a priest, people often confide in me to share things and ask for advice. When people have something to say, it's important to listen. Sometimes people just need to get things off their chest. Priests see a lot and have experience, which makes them good at giving advice. So, if you have a secret that needs to be confessed, I pray and hope that you find a way to bring it to Confession.

In the Gospel of Mark, we see that Jesus had a secret. Whenever he cast out a demon, the demon would reveal that Jesus was the Son of David, the Holy One of God. Jesus would call that infernal being to silence. Anytime someone would reveal that Jesus was the Messiah, especially in the Gospel of Mark, Jesus would usually ask them not to tell anyone, except for one place.

Do you know where Jesus revealed himself as the Messiah in Mark's gospel? It was on the Cross, where a Roman soldier, a pagan, said, "Truly this man was the Son of God" (Mark 15:39). This is where the Messianic secret was revealed.

In the Gospel of John, Jesus revealed himself to a Samaritan woman. Not just any Samaritan woman, but one who had not had the best luck in her love life. He revealed himself to her as a way to reveal himself to us. He said, "I who speak to you am the Messiah, the Anointed One: Christ, the one who was sent."

In times of anxiety, fear, and uncertainty, when things seem to be falling apart, it's important to remember that Jesus is here. He is the Christ, and he is saying to you, "I am here to turn your problems and worries over to me." Give your anxieties over to him, and stop trying to control everything. Allow Jesus to take control of your life.

REFLECT

1. Do you have a secret or something on your conscience that you need to bring to the Sacrament of Confession? Do you value this sacrament as an encounter with God's healing mercy and love?
2. Jesus revealed his identity to the Samaritan woman. What does this tell you about his love for those who are on the margins of society or who feel lost in sin?
3. How can you turn your anxieties and concerns over to Jesus in trust?

_____

_____

_____

_____

_____

_____

PRAY

_LORD, HOW OFTEN WHEN I AM GOING
THROUGH SOMETHING, I EITHER
KEEP IT TO MYSELF, FEELING ALL
ALONE WITH IT, OR SOMETIMES I
COMPLAIN TO EVERYONE I MEET!
GIVE ME THE GRACE TO FIRST
CONFIDE IN YOU AND TO SURRENDER
MY CONCERN TO YOU. PLEASE SEND
ME A GOOD ADVISOR WHO I CAN
TRUST WILL HELP ME FIND YOUR WILL
AND NOT JUST SAY WHAT I WANT TO
HEAR! HELP ME TO PLACE ALL MY
TRUST IN YOU._

FOURTH WEEK
OF LENT

BECOME A
VESSEL OF
GOD'S LOVE

FOURTH WEEK OF LENT

SUNDAY

AS HE PASSED BY, HE SAW A MAN
BLIND FROM HIS BIRTH. AND HIS
DISCIPLES ASKED HIM, "RABBI,
WHO SINNED, THIS MAN OR HIS
PARENTS, THAT HE WAS BORN
BLIND?" JESUS ANSWERED,
"IT WAS NOT THAT THIS MAN
SINNED, OR HIS PARENTS, BUT
THAT THE WORKS OF GOD MIGHT
BE MADE MANIFEST IN HIM."

JOHN 9:1–3

LEARNING TO TRUST GOD

We all have an innate sense of what is right and wrong; even children have this "playground" sense of justice, which is a good thing. However, this natural sense of justice needs to be informed by what Jesus taught us. There is a need to embrace the depth of God's mercy, which can sometimes challenge this sense of justice. Let me be clear: God does not contradict himself, but what to some might seem to be a lack of justice could be an outpouring of mercy to others.

As followers of Jesus, we need to strive to be more like him, especially in this way. The disciples believed that the man's blindness was punishment for some wrongdoing, just as we often think that those who suffer are being punished for some mistake they made. If it's not their fault, then it must have been the fault of their parents or grandparents.

In truth, we do suffer from the actions of our loved ones. Perhaps you have heard someone say, "They made me this way." Our actions do impact those around us, but blaming others is not how Jesus teaches us to approach things. Instead, we must learn to forgive and show mercy, just as Jesus did. Remember, even in our darkest moments, God's love and mercy shines through.

Jesus explained that the man's blindness was an opportunity for God's glory to be revealed. Our lives are filled with trials and tribulations, even those that carry down to us from long ago. These experiences can be painful, but they can also provide an opportunity for transformation and healing. What happened to us—whether in our childhood or later years—can be used by God for a greater purpose. While we may not understand why events unfolded as they did, God has the power to bring goodness from them.

To become stronger in our faith and lead others, we must first undergo a personal transformation. This transformation is more about trusting God than about being healed. To be healed is good and part of the process, but the ultimate goal is about strengthening our trust and connection with God. It is not just about receiving comfort but being in the presence of Jesus. We must be willing to allow God's love to open our hearts and transform us. Every saint went through their trials and allowed God to work through those difficulties. We too should surrender ourselves to be transformed by growing in trust.

Instead of dwelling on assigning fault for our past issues, we should embrace the fact that, through our brokenness, God has the ability to manifest glory in our lives. Today, consider how God wishes to enter your life and heal your past wounds by illuminating a new path forward—one that is grounded in faith and allows his glory to shine through you.

REFLECT

1. Do you ever feel challenged by God's call to pursue mercy and compassion in your dealings with others?
2. How can you surrender your trials to God, trusting that he accompanies you through each challenging moment?
3. How might a particular trial in your life be an opportunity for God's love to be shown?

PRAY

*LORD, TRY AS I MAY TO PRAY
ANOTHER WAY, I OFTEN BEGIN WITH
MY HURTS AND PAINS. I ASK YOU TO
HEAL ME BECAUSE THE PAIN I FEEL IS
OFTEN BEYOND ANY REMEDY I KNOW
OF. PLEASE HELP ME, LORD. I WANT
TO MOVE BEYOND JUST NEEDING TO
BE HEALED, BUT I MUST BEGIN BY
BEING HEALED. I LONG TO BE MORE
OF WHAT YOU WANT ME TO BE, BUT I
START AND STOP AGAIN AND AGAIN.
LORD, HAVE MERCY ON ME AND HELP
ME TO TAKE THE NEXT STEP.*

FOURTH WEEK OF LENT

MONDAY

"WE MUST WORK THE WORKS
OF HIM WHO SENT ME, WHILE
IT IS DAY; NIGHT COMES, WHEN
NO ONE CAN WORK. AS LONG
AS I AM IN THE WORLD, I AM
THE LIGHT OF THE WORLD." AS
HE SAID THIS, HE SPAT ON THE
GROUND AND MADE CLAY OF
THE SPITTLE AND ANOINTED
THE MAN'S EYES WITH THE CLAY.

JOHN 9:4–6

BELIEVING WHEN
WE CANNOT SEE

In sacred scripture there is meaning in everything Jesus says and does. First of all, this passage starts out with the message that Jesus has been sent by the Father. Then Jesus *proclaims* that he has been sent and acts on his mission by signs and wonders. After such a bold claim, one would think that the next action is of increased significance. What does Jesus do next? He spits, puts clay on the man's eyes, and tells him to go wash in a pool called Siloam. Then the man reacts: first he is blind, then he obeys, and finally he is able to see.

What was the "active agent" that caused this man to see? In those times, saliva was a folk remedy for blindness. We know this from the ancient Roman writings of Pliny the Younger and Suetonius. It's probably safe to say that people had already tried to spit on the blind man and wash him. That's why he was there near the pool. None of it worked until Jesus did it, but Jesus isn't some sort of folk healer. In fact, this is such a rich story because there are a number of ways to draw meaning from it.

St. John Chrysostom said that the saliva signifies the Word of God. Just as Jesus the Word was sent from God, the saliva came from Jesus's mouth and fell to the ground, where it was mixed with the material of earth. Some of the other church fathers say that when Jesus was mixing the saliva with the earth to form clay, it was like going back to the first creation, where God formed Adam.

Think of mission here too. Jesus was sent to be light to the world, then he sent the man to wash in the pool, where he was healed. The pool was called Siloam, which means "sent." So there's a clear chain of imagery in this story that we need to pay attention to.

Blindness in the New Testament is often a metaphor for sinfulness or for lack of faith. All of these things mean that when we act like this man—when we recognize that we are blind, and we obey when God speaks—God will restore our sight. Not only that, but he will also *send us* to participate in his mission.

Do you want to fulfill God's will? If this is something that is on your heart, pray for that burning desire to take the next step. You will see that there are many areas in your heart that are blind because of a lack of faith or sin, but when you obey him and reconcile—when you forgive and are forgiven—you will see.

REFLECT

1. Are there areas of blindness in your own life? How can you follow Jesus's call to wash and be clean, to forgive and receive forgiveness?
2. Just as Jesus was sent by the Father, he sends each of us, too, to share the Good News with others. How do feel about this call, and how might you better follow it?
3. Is there something on your heart with which you feel God is calling you to take the next step to fulfill his will? How can you move forward this Lent?

PRAY

*LORD, I LONG TO SEE YOUR FACE.
THE MANY TIMES I HAVE LACKED
FAITH HAVE DIMMED MY SIGHT. MY
MANY RATIONALIZATIONS HAVE KEPT
ME FROM THE SIMPLE CONSOLATION
OF KNOWING THAT ALL THINGS
WILL BE WELL IN YOUR HOLY NAME.
LORD, YOU TRULY HEAR MY PRAYERS.
YOU TRULY RESPOND. FORGIVE THE
TIMES I HAVE FALLEN BACK WHEN MY
CONSOLATION DID NOT COME WHEN
I DESIRED IT. FORGIVE MY NEED TO
FEEL YOUR PROMISE FULFILLED. HELP
ME TO KNOW THAT YOUR HEALING
TOUCH WILL COME.*

FOURTH WEEK OF LENT

TUESDAY

THE NEIGHBORS AND THOSE WHO HAD
SEEN HIM BEFORE AS A BEGGAR, SAID,
"IS NOT THIS THE MAN WHO USED
TO SIT AND BEG?" SOME SAID, "IT IS
HE"; OTHERS SAID, "NO, BUT HE IS
LIKE HIM." HE SAID, "I AM THE MAN."
THEY SAID TO HIM, "THEN HOW WERE
YOUR EYES OPENED?" HE ANSWERED,
"THE MAN CALLED JESUS MADE CLAY
AND ANOINTED MY EYES AND SAID TO
ME, 'GO TO SILOAM AND WASH'; SO I
WENT AND WASHED AND RECEIVED MY
SIGHT." THEY SAID TO HIM, "WHERE IS
HE?" HE SAID, "I DO NOT KNOW."

JOHN 9:8–12

BECOME A VESSEL OF MERCY

Should not there have been a celebration if a man born blind recovered his sight? Do we recognize who God is healing around us?

One time, at our friary in the Bronx, a knock came at the door. A brother called for me to speak to a man covered in tattoos. He had an intense look about him, but then again so do most people in our neighborhood. He asked for thirty dollars to get a tattoo. I laughed and said, "That is one I have never heard before. What is your story?"

As he spoke, I realized I had seen him before at a local Catholic conference. I had gone to hear Confessions at this event, and there he was. This young man went up on the stage and fell on his knees with his arms outstretched. He was a member of a notorious gang, but as he came to embrace the teachings of Jesus Christ, he was forced to leave. He had been going through a spiritual transformation, but to leave the gang he had to leave everything, and he had been living on the streets ever since. They finally gave him special permission to leave (without retribution), but they demanded he remove a tattoo as a condition of his departure. This tattoo was a mark on his inner lip.

He was running out of time and needed help. He told me he had been to every church in the Bronx looking for thirty dollars to cover the tattoo of his now-former gang, but everyone turned him away. He said, "You Christians say you help people, but everyone has turned their back on me." We would not turn him away. I went myself to negotiate the price at the tattoo parlor. He left the gang and instead joined a Bible study group. The way he had been treated reminded me of the story of the blind man. After being healed, he was shut out by those who should have celebrated his healing.

This man in the gospel account was healed, and the religious leaders and his family were callously uncaring or actively fighting against him. Perhaps you, too, are experiencing a similar moment of unshackling and upheaval in your life, and the Church has left you feeling disenchanted and wounded. Maybe you are the empathetic soul that seeks to aid and comfort such people. Whatever the circumstance, it is our Christian duty to offer mercy, love, and compassion to all we encounter.

It is important that we remember that grace is active and flowing, and it is incumbent upon us as believers to spread it to those who need it most. There is no moment too small or insignificant or ordinary to be an opportunity for grace to break in! To live the way of Christ, we must seek out those in need continually. May we all remember that we are vessels of mercy, and it is our divine duty to pour this mercy out in every interaction we have with others.

REFLECT

1. How can you become a vessel of mercy in everyday circumstances with your family, friends, or community?
2. Do you celebrate and rejoice with others who have experienced God's healing in some way?
3. Is there an opportunity for you to participate more fully in your parish community by accompanying others in their faith and sharing this company yourself?

PRAY

*LORD, I THANK YOU FOR BRINGING
ME THOSE WHO HAVE BEEN HEALED
AND ARE HEALING. GRANT ME A
DESIRE TO WELCOME THOSE WHO
HAVE BEEN WOUNDED BY THE
TIMES AND THEIR CIRCUMSTANCES.
LORD, GIVE ME THE GRACE AND
PATIENCE TO LISTEN TO THEM. TO
HEAR THEIR STORY. TO LOVE WHERE
THEY ARE FROM, NO MATTER HOW
DIFFERENT IT MAY BE FROM MY OWN
EXPERIENCE. HELP ME BE HEALED BY
BRINGING HEALING.*

FOURTH WEEK OF LENT

WEDNESDAY

THE WORD BECAME FLESH AND
DWELT AMONG US.

JOHN 1:14

LET THE WORD
BECOME FLESH IN YOU

One of my favorite places to pray in New York City is in the Cloisters in the Metropolitan Museum of Art in Upper Manhattan. Over the years the museum has accumulated some amazing medieval art, and it is housed now in a monastery-shaped museum. One of these incredible works of art is the Mèrode Altarpiece—which can be viewed here: https://bit.ly/madeforheavenart—a triptych that depicts the Annunciation; the piece dates to the 1400s. It is truly a world-class masterpiece.

The altarpiece depicts the moment the angel Gabriel appeared to Mary, hailed her as "full of grace," and invited her to receive the Holy Spirit so that Jesus could be incarnate in her womb. Then she said, "I am the handmaid of the Lord; let it be to me according to your word" (Luke 1:38). This "yes" changed history. Today, we have the chance to say the same "yes" to the grace being given us to enter into the story of Jesus. Let me explain.

A triptych is a three-panel work of art that would adorn altars and open when the priest would celebrate Holy Mass. The Mèrode Altarpiece is Gothic in style and of the Netherland school of that period. The center panel shows the Annunciation, the panel to the right shows Joseph in his workshop, and the panel to the left shows the donors who commissioned the work. It might seem a bit rash to include yourself in the work of art you paid for, but their inclusion is good theology. Would that we all would want to be included in the benefits of the Incarnation!

There are so many little details in this work of art. The center panel is absolutely mystifying with its colors and textures. Mary is dressed in a vivid red as she reads the scriptures, which follows a tradition that when the angel appeared to her, she was in prayer. The angel Gabriel is appearing before her through the glass. Through the window, there's a little baby Jesus riding the wave of the Holy Spirit about to enter into the womb of our Blessed Mother. St. Joseph is in his workshop hammering away, making a mousetrap. St. Augustine says that the Cross was the wood that functioned like a mousetrap that caught the devil and destroyed death forever.

For our meditation, let us gaze upon Mary reading the scriptures so that the Word of God would be made flesh in her. When we read the Word of God something happens in us as well. Mary said yes to receiving the Word of God in her reading, and this prepared her to receive the Word-made-flesh in her womb. This was a decision that had profound implications for all of us.

The same thing happens when we give ourselves to prayer and let the Word of God take flesh in us. We have the opportunity to bear Jesus to others too. So let's try to act like the donors who commissioned this painting; let's try to get as close as we can to that moment so that we, too, may enter into the story of the Incarnation. Today, meditate on the Word so that the Word can become flesh in you.

REFLECT

1. How can you say "yes" to the Word of God as you read or hear the scriptures, just as Mary did?
2. Look up the Mèrode Altarpiece and consider the art and meaning described here and anything else that speaks to you. How does this piece of art inspire you to follow Jesus, the Word-made-flesh?
3. What do you think of St. Augustine's description of the wood of the Cross as a mousetrap for the devil?

PRAY

*LORD, YOU CALLED SO MANY TO BE
A PART OF YOUR SALVATION. JESUS,
DEEPEN THE DESIRE OF MY HEART
TO WANT MORE OF YOUR LOVE.
OFTEN WORRIES AND DISTRACTIONS
ABOUND AND TAKE ME AWAY FROM
THE CENTER OF WORSHIP. DRAW
MY HEART INTO THIS DRAMA OF
SALVATION. FOR MYSELF, FOR
OTHERS, FOR MY FAMILY, FOR THE
FORGOTTEN, DRAW ME DEEPER INTO
PRAYER FOR YOUR HEALING GRACE.*

FOURTH WEEK OF LENT

THURSDAY

THEY HELD STEADFASTLY TO
THE APOSTLES' TEACHING AND
FELLOWSHIP. . . . AND ALL WHO
BELIEVED WERE TOGETHER AND HAD
ALL THINGS IN COMMON; AND THEY
SOLD THEIR POSSESSIONS AND GOODS
AND DISTRIBUTED THEM TO ALL,
AS ANY HAD NEED. AND DAY BY DAY,
ATTENDING THE TEMPLE TOGETHER
AND BREAKING BREAD IN THEIR
HOMES, THEY PARTOOK OF FOOD
WITH GLAD AND GENEROUS HEARTS,
PRAISING GOD AND HAVING FAVOR
WITH ALL THE PEOPLE. AND THE LORD
ADDED TO THEIR NUMBER DAY BY DAY
THOSE WHO WERE BEING SAVED.

ACTS 2:42–47

A SINCERE HEART

We began our Lenten journey by remembering the practices of the first Christians and how from the very start they gathered on Sundays to remember the Lord's Resurrection. It is instructive to return to those roots, to see how people responded to Jesus's life, death, and Resurrection before they had a global institution to show them the way. In this passage from the Acts of the Apostles, we get another glimpse into our ancestors in faith.

Their experience of Jesus and the new life of his Resurrection gave them a new way to live. We see here that they were not afraid of departing from the mainstream, of being countercultural. Not only did they gather regularly to break bread and pray together (sounds just like Sunday Mass, doesn't it!), they also held things in common. Just as we are doing on our Lenten journey, they embraced a practice of poverty and simple living. They went so far as to sell what they had so they could pool their resources and share them within the community so that everyone had what they needed.

These first Christians were so focused and on fire with the Good News that they ordered their whole lives around it together. Their experience of the risen Lord in their community came first—they fit everything else around that. And guess what? People noticed! Every day, their numbers grew. Every day, someone in the city saw the way they were living and decided to also go all-in on the Gospel. These early Christians lived in such a way that neighbors and friends and coworkers and shop owners and extended family couldn't help but notice. So they asked why they had made those choices, and the Christians spoke of Jesus with sincere joy. And all those people thought, "They have found something I want!"

There is a desire for God burning inside each one of us. If we can live our communion with God and one another boldly, we will ignite that fire in others. Let us pray for faithfulness, for courage, and for generosity so that the light of the Gospel shines through our lives and lights a way for others to find the Good News that has saved us.

REFLECT

1. Do you sometimes struggle with being countercultural? How can you find inspiration in the early Christians' devotion to their new life of faith and service after the Resurrection?
2. Have you ever encountered a Christian who seemed to have a special joy about them? Did they inspire you to follow Christ more closely?
3. How might you live with more generosity toward others?

PRAY

*LORD, HELP ME TO FOLLOW YOU
LIKE THE EARLY CHRISTIANS. FILL
MY HEART WITH SO MUCH LOVE FOR
YOU THAT IT TRANSFORMS MY LIFE.
MAY MY LIFE BE A LIGHT THAT SHINES
FORTH WITH YOUR LOVE, LEADING
OTHERS TO YOU.*

FOURTH WEEK OF LENT

FRIDAY

THE APPOINTED TIME HAS GROWN
VERY SHORT; FROM NOW ON, LET
THOSE WHO HAVE WIVES LIVE AS
THOUGH THEY HAD NONE, AND THOSE
WHO MOURN AS THOUGH THEY WERE
NOT MOURNING, AND THOSE WHO
REJOICE AS THOUGH THEY WERE NOT
REJOICING, AND THOSE WHO BUY AS
THOUGH THEY HAD NO GOODS, AND
THOSE WHO DEAL WITH THE WORLD AS
THOUGH THEY HAD NO DEALINGS WITH
IT. FOR THE FORM OF THIS WORLD IS
PASSING AWAY.

I CORINTHIANS 7:29–31

POVERTY CHECK—
LETTING GO OF
ATTACHMENTS

In this passage from Paul's letter to the Corinthians, he gives us all a reminder: no matter what we are experiencing—whether it is good or bad—we have to keep our focus on Jesus.

Our lives are soaked with worldly worries. We are occupied all the time with things that we experience as good and bad: Traffic is heavy. Someone gave me a compliment. I'm worried about the future. I got paid today. These kinds of occupations are not good or bad in and of themselves, but they do take up our time and our focus on what is most necessary.

What is most necessary? Our lives are passing away, but we are created for heaven. Our task is to become aware of what we cling to so we can become more detached and focused on our practice of poverty as a call to the eternal, as a pathway toward union with God. That means that our practice of poverty must be a constant process of conversion.

Without realizing it, we grow in attachment to things that are ultimately not necessary. Many relationships we have and possessions are good, and we praise God for them. Then there are those that are not, and they weigh on us. If you are consumed with an object or relationship, you may have an attitude of appropriation or attachment. Consider what you cling to and why you may have this attitude.

How can you grow in poverty of spirit and imitate the heart of Christ? Avoid complaining about what you don't have, and strive to be content with the minimum necessary. Grow in trust of our Heavenly Father and his divine providence. Do not consider yourself above anyone. Consider if there is anything that you ought to give away.

The practice of poverty should be a little unsettling because it should always raise our eyes to something else. It helps to ponder these questions and share them with a friend or with your family in discussion.

REFLECT

1. How does recalling your mortality and the promise of eternity change your perspective? How can you live with more focus on God rather than on merely worldly concerns?
2. What do you find yourself overly concerned with or spending too much time on at the expense of more important things? How is God calling you to detach from this in order to serve him more fully?
3. What is one simple and practical way you can exercise detachment from something this week (less screen time, giving something away, saying no to buying something new, etc.)

PRAY

LORD, ONLY YOU WILL SATISFY. MY HEART IS RESTLESS UNTIL IT RESTS IN YOU. BUT I HAVE TRIED TO FULFILL THE RESTLESSNESS IN SO MANY WAYS. YOU CONSTANTLY REACH OUT TO ME, NEVER ABANDONING ME, NEVER GIVING UP ON ME. LORD, GIVE ME THE GRACE TO ROOT UP UNHEALTHY ATTACHMENTS. GO GENTLY, LORD, FOR I HAVE MANY. LET YOUR HOLY WILL BE DONE IN ME.

FOURTH WEEK OF LENT

SATURDAY

AND A GREAT STORM OF WIND
AROSE, AND THE WAVES BEAT
INTO THE BOAT, SO THAT THE
BOAT WAS ALREADY FILLING. BUT
HE WAS IN THE STERN, ASLEEP
ON THE CUSHION; AND THEY
WOKE HIM AND SAID TO HIM,
"TEACHER, DO YOU NOT CARE
IF WE PERISH?" AND HE AWOKE
AND REBUKED THE WIND, AND
SAID TO THE SEA, "PEACE! BE
STILL!" AND THE WIND CEASED,
AND THERE WAS A GREAT CALM.

MARK 4:37–39

JESUS CALMS THE STORM

Jesus and his disciples were in a boat when a storm started to rage. The ship was tossed around and the disciples feared for their lives. They cried out, "Do you not care if we perish?"

One might wonder why Jesus was sleeping when all this was happening. This may be the only time we hear of Jesus sleeping. When we face difficulties in our lives today, we may feel that Jesus is asleep and not paying attention to our struggles. (Have you ever thought that Jesus is a deep sleeper? I've wondered about that myself!)

When the disciples asked, "Do you not care?" it seems that they were reacting not just to the current situation but also to past disappointments that still hurt them. We may be like the disciples, whose faith was still growing. Perhaps we need these storms to learn to believe more deeply. After they saw Jesus calm the storm, the disciples were prompted to ask, "Who is this?" (see Mark 4:41).

We are being tossed about by storms of wars, storms of environmental issues, storms of politics, storms of our own wounds. Could it be that these storms are in some way necessary to soften our hearts? Is there a wound from the past that is not allowing us to have faith, and through the storm we will see more of who Jesus is? In the midst of our own storms, God reveals his heart to us. Let us also pray to know Jesus more deeply in our hearts and to trust him always.

Pope Francis commented on this scene, "In this storm, the façade of those stereotypes with which we camouflaged our egos, always worrying about our image, has fallen away, uncovering once more that (blessed) common belonging, of which we cannot be deprived: our belonging as brothers and sisters" (*Urbi et Orbi*, March 27, 2020).

To be concerned about others during whatever storms are breaking upon us is a sign that Jesus is alive. You might say this kind of generosity is a virtue of humanity. What is the camouflage that is being uncovered in our storm? Perhaps we never reached out to say, "Hey, you guys have everything that you need? Do you need anything?" This is not an easy thing to do when we are feeling tossed around, or when we know in the back of our heads that we only have precious little, ourselves.

Right now there are those in our communities who are in despair and feel as the disciples. They say, "God doesn't care. He is asleep." But our concern and prayers are indeed powerful. We need to be praying for them so that a storm may be an occasion for the deepening of their faith.

REFLECT

1. Do you ever feel as if Jesus is asleep in the midst of your struggles or moments of suffering?
2. How can you grow in faith like the apostles, knowing that Jesus is always with you and wants you to trust in him?
3. In a special way this week, can you pray for those who feel lost or forsaken in a storm of life, asking that God strengthen them and help them recognize his presence and grace?

_____

_____

_____

_____

PRAY

_LORD, I BELIEVE; HELP MY UNBELIEF.
I BELIEVE IN YOU, BUT I AM
WOUNDED FROM ALL THE TIMES THAT
I WEATHERED STORMS AND I DID NOT
FEEL YOU CLOSE. I KNOW YOU WERE
CLOSE, BUT AT THE TIME I DID NOT
FEEL YOU CLOSE. I KNOW YOU WERE
CARRYING ME. NOW AT THIS TIME I
ASK THAT THAT KNOWLEDGE MOVE
DOWN TO MY HEART. LORD, LET IT
TRAVEL THE LONGEST JOURNEY FROM
THE HEAD TO THE HEART. ALLOW
MY TRUST TO GROW WHEN ANOTHER
STORM RAGES. YOU WILL CALM IT
AS YOU DID EVERY OTHER ONE. IF I
HAVE FELT YOU ASLEEP, I KNOW IT IS
SO THAT MY TRUST IN YOU COULD
GROW. THANK YOU, LORD._

FIFTH WEEK
OF LENT

RISE TO NEW LIFE

SO THE SISTERS SENT TO HIM,
SAYING, "LORD, HE WHOM YOU
LOVE IS ILL."

JOHN 11:3

PRAYING WITH CONFIDENCE

Martha and Mary, the sisters of Lazarus, offer a valuable lesson on how to pray with confidence, knowing that God will answer our prayers. According to the gospel, the sisters sent a simple message to Jesus: "Lord, he whom you love is ill." They did not provide specific instructions or demands for how Jesus should act, but rather presented the situation to him in faith. And Jesus, upon hearing their prayer, responded by assuring them that the sickness would not end in death, but instead bring glory to God. Although the sisters did not initially hear Jesus's answer, their prayer was answered because they had presented the situation to him in faith.

Perhaps we could follow their example and pray in a similar way. It might be shocking how our prayers are often focused on ourselves. What does it look like to pray and trust that Jesus will act, even if we do not know or do not have control over what he will do? Instead of listing all our requests to God—all the things *we* think God should do to solve our problems—we can simply present each situation to him with faith, confident that he will act on our behalf.

Mary did the same thing at the wedding at Cana. She saw what was happening as the wedding party was running out of wine and pointed it out to Jesus. She didn't tell him how to fix it—she probably couldn't imagine him changing water to wine—but she just knew he would respond to the need in a way that reveals God's kingdom. That's what he did.

When we are facing problems and challenges, we can simply share our need with God and then wait in faith. We don't need to tell God what to do. By praying this way, we are acknowledging that we trust God to do what is best in each situation.

So, I encourage you to pray in this manner today, to go through your prayer list and present each request to God with faith, knowing and trusting that he will act. When we present our needs to him, he will do the rest.

REFLECT

1. Do you often pray to God in a way that directs him to act in the way you wish? How can you better trust his ways over your own?

2. What can you learn from Martha and Mary about praying with confidence that God will act?

3. Is there a particular prayer request that you can put forth to God today in a spirit of trust, knowing he will fulfill that prayer in the best way, even if it's not in the way you expect?

_____

_____

_____

_____

_____

_____

_____

_____

_____

_____

_____

_____

_____

_____

_____

_____

_____

PRAY

_LORD, THERE ARE MANY PEOPLE IN
MY HEART THAT I BRING TO YOU. I
PRAY FOR THEM WITH ALL I HAVE.
PLEASE, LORD, RECEIVE THEM. I
ENTRUST THEM TO YOU. THE ONES
WHOM YOU LOVE ARE SICK, HURTING,
DOUBTING, DRIFTING, ANGRY,
AND LONELY. THEY ARE WOUNDED,
CONFUSED, AND LACKING TRUST. I
KNOW YOU WILL ACT. I BELIEVE IN
THE RESURRECTION AND IN YOUR
HEALING GRACE. AMEN._

FIFTH WEEK OF LENT

MONDAY

NOW JESUS LOVED MARTHA
AND HER SISTER AND LAZ'ARUS.
SO WHEN HE HEARD THAT HE
WAS ILL, HE STAYED TWO DAYS
LONGER IN THE PLACE WHERE
HE WAS.

JOHN 11:5-6

TRUSTING HIM EVERMORE

I had a good friend who was an artist in the city. She worked on films and often helped me when I was in charge of organizing plays about the life of St. Francis. The friars would invite people to come, and she would assist me in managing the production. She was a wonderful person and had even been a religious sister for a while, though she eventually realized that was not her true calling. She lived on her own, and when she reached forty, she thought she would be single forever. But she always had a smile on her face and remained open to what the Lord was doing in her life. Her love of Jesus grew, and she trusted in his plan, even if things didn't work out the way she at first thought. Her focus was on the Resurrection.

Then one day, she met someone and got married at the age of forty. To her surprise, she became pregnant soon after. She did not understand why the Lord had done things in that way, but she was overjoyed and wanted God to be glorified through her experience. Looking back now, it is easy to say that everything worked out well, but it was difficult for her to wait and be patient during that time.

Similarly, when Jesus waited for two days before going to see Lazarus, Martha, and Mary, people wondered why he did not act immediately. Jesus said he waited so that the glory of God may be seen through their situation. Perhaps the reason God has not answered your prayers immediately or in the way you expected is that he wants to be glorified through your experience. Perhaps our trust needs to grow and our faith in the Resurrection needs to become more central in our lives. These are not easy lessons to learn, but life has a way of bringing them to us.

My friend who got married at forty and later had a baby seemed to be living her dream life in Brooklyn. Eight years later, however, she was diagnosed with brain cancer. Despite the difficult circumstances, she remained faithful to God and gave everything to him, even her life. Her husband had grown close to God through his marriage. Though she passed away, I know that God will continue to bless her widower and young daughter because of her unwavering faith. Of course they miss her, but her faith is still an inspiration. It is a gift that reaches beyond death—it touched her family and it touched me. Now I share it with you. The faithfulness of this wife and mother is still bearing fruit in the world.

Even if God does not respond to your prayers in the way you desire, he is still acting, and we should pray to trust him more and wait on the Lord to act, for he will act.

REFLECT

1. What thoughts and feelings arise for you as you consider the story of this woman who married later in life and then died from brain cancer? How does she inspire you to trust God amid life's ups and downs?

2. Have you ever had a time of suffering but then recognized how you grew and God was glorified through that situation? What have you learned from that experience?

3. Are you surprised when you read this scripture that Jesus did not come immediately to heal his friend Lazarus? What lessons do you learn from this story?

_____

_____

_____

_____

PRAY

*LORD, I STRUGGLE WHEN I
HAVE TO WAIT. I AM A MUCH
MORE PLEASANT PERSON WHEN
EVERYTHING HAPPENS WHEN I
WANT. FORGIVE MY SELFISHNESS,
LORD. I REPENT FOR THE TIMES I
GREW ANGRY FOR NOT GETTING
MY WAY. THERE WERE TIMES I
PRAYED AND ASKED FOR WHAT I
WANTED, AND YOU GRANTED ME
THE MERCY TO WAIT. THANK YOU,
LORD, FOR THE WAIT. THANK
YOU, LORD, FOR THE GIFT OF THE
DESERT OF EXPECTATION, FOR
IN THE BARENESS I CANNOT HIDE
BEHIND MY DEFENSES. THE SUBTLE
STING OF MY VANITY IS SOOTHED
BY THE BRIGHTNESS OF THE STARS
IN THIS DESERT OF WAITING. I
WAIT FOR YOU, LORD.*

FIFTH WEEK OF LENT

TUESDAY

THEN AFTER THIS HE SAID TO THE DISCIPLES, "LET US GO INTO JUDEA AGAIN." THE DISCIPLES SAID TO HIM, "RABBI, THE JEWS WERE BUT NOW SEEKING TO STONE YOU, AND ARE YOU GOING THERE AGAIN?" . . . THEN HE SAID TO THEM, "OUR FRIEND LAZ'ARUS HAS FALLEN ASLEEP, BUT I GO TO AWAKE HIM OUT OF SLEEP."

JOHN 11:7–8, 11

STEPPING OUT IN FAITH

I recently had a conversation with a young single mother who seemed to be considering aborting her baby. She already had a little daughter, and she was overwhelmed. Her family supported her, but everyone agreed that she needed more balance. I asked her how she was doing, and she said that it was hard. She said, "Everyone talks about pro-life and pro-choice positions, but when you are in a real-life situation, you're the one who has to live with it every day." I agreed with her and told her that she was the most pro-life person I had met. She was living the day-to-day of what it means to choose life. Moment by moment, she was sustaining her new child, even though it was a struggle. I thanked her for her life and her family. She smiled and said that having her daughter was the best thing she had ever done, even though it was difficult. She loves her daughter more than anything.

In a sense, she was in a tomb like Lazarus—she felt closed in by darkness, in a cold, hard place without any light coming in. She was expressing how difficult it was to wait without knowing how things could work out. But she was being guided by the light of her love for her daughter; that was one place of warmth for her. So there she was, in the dark, but waiting for God to break into her experience. This is what I meant by her being pro-life: she was living with real hope that, in some way, God would bring her new life.

If God is asking you to do something, know that he will confirm it. He is a good Father who loves his children. He will not leave us in the dark. His invitation is from a deep well of love. He does ask us to get out of our comfort zone, however, for how could we ever grow if we stay in one place? He asks us to go to places within our heart that are difficult to see. If you are facing a situation that you can't see through and it doesn't make sense, if you know it's from him, go for it. Don't be afraid or overthink it. Follow the Lord, and see what great things he can do with your little step of faith.

REFLECT

1. Where is God calling you to move out of your comfort zone? How does he promise that you will grow by doing so?
2. What inspires you about the woman who gives life to her children while hoping that God will accompany her through her situation? What can you learn from her and apply to your own life?
3. Can you accompany someone who is in a challenging situation, not only through prayer, but also by assisting them in some practical ways?

_____

_____

_____

_____

_____

_____

_____

_____

PRAY

_LORD JESUS, TO FOLLOW YOU TAKES
ME PLACES THAT ARE DIFFICULT
TO GO. LORD, IN MY LITTLENESS
I WOULD RATHER STAY WHERE IT
IS SAFE. IT SEEMS AS IF WHEN I
HAVE FINALLY GOTTEN USED TO
SOMETHING OR FEEL COMFORTABLE
WITH A PLACE OR SITUATION,
EVERYTHING CHANGES. LORD, HELP
ME FOLLOW YOU WHEREVER YOU GO._

FIFTH WEEK OF LENT

WEDNESDAY

MARTHA SAID TO JESUS, "LORD,
IF YOU HAD BEEN HERE, MY
BROTHER WOULD NOT HAVE
DIED. AND EVEN NOW I KNOW
THAT WHATEVER YOU ASK FROM
GOD, GOD WILL GIVE YOU."

JOHN 11:21–22

TENDING THE LITTLE THINGS

Thank you, Martha, for your hospitality and welcoming nature. When Jesus arrived, you didn't hesitate to go to him. It's inspiring to see how natural it was for you to run to Jesus and open your heart to him. Your words to Jesus show a deep prayer life and a radical disposition of trust. We can all learn from your example and pray with the same trust, saying, "Lord, wherever you lead me, I will follow you. Lord, whatever you ask me, I will do."

There is a famous poem by Henry Wadsworth Longfellow called "The Theologian's Tale; The Legend Beautiful." In it, he tells of a friar who was deep in prayer when suddenly Jesus appeared to him. The friar was in ecstasy, overwhelmed by the sight of the Lord, and he began to adore him. In the midst of his vision, however, there was a knock at the door, and the friar had to pause to answer it. Despite his disappointment at being interrupted, he knew it was his responsibility to attend to whomever was at the door. When he opened the door, he found a man covered in sores, who was poor and hungry. The friar immediately tended to the man's needs by giving him food and water, treating his wounds, and giving him something to wear. He then returned to the chapel, exhausted but fulfilled, for it was his duty to serve others. To his surprise, when he arrived back at the chapel, he found that Jesus was waiting for him. The friar fell to his knees, and he heard Jesus say, "If you had stayed, I would have gone." His act of service was an outgrowth of his prayer. It flowed from the chapel to the streets. This experience taught the friar the importance of being faithful in his responsibilities and in serving others, even if it meant interrupting his own personal experiences.

Martha was a person of prayer as well, and she trusted that Jesus would come and help her brother. She believed even beyond death. So, let us all be like Martha, with a deep prayer life and a radical disposition of trust, and be faithful in the little things, knowing that God will do great things for us.

REFLECT

1. What inspires you in the poem about the friar who left his prayer to serve a sick man? How are prayer and service interlinked?
2. How can you follow Martha's example of both service and prayerful trust in God in both big and small things?
3. How can you practice hospitality in your family, workplace, or community this Lent?

_____

_____

_____

_____

_____

PRAY

*MY PRAYER, MY LORD, IS OFTEN
DISTRACTED. WHEN I TRY TO PRAY,
THOUGHTS OF EVERYTHING ELSE
COME TO MY MIND. IT SEEMS AS IF
IN MASS I AM MORE DISTRACTED
THAN OUTSIDE OF CHURCH. IN THE
QUIETING OF MY SURROUNDINGS,
THE NOISE OF WHAT IS NOT RIGHT
OR WHAT I STILL HAVE TO DO GROWS
LOUDER. YOU TAUGHT MARTHA TO
FOCUS ON THE BETTER THINGS.
HELP ME, LORD, TO SET ASIDE WHAT
I THINK NEEDS TO HAPPEN SO I CAN
CONTEMPLATE YOU BEFORE ME. YOU
ARE ENOUGH, LORD.*

FIFTH WEEK OF LENT

THURSDAY

WHEN SHE HAD SAID THIS,
SHE WENT AND CALLED HER
SISTER MARY, SAYING QUIETLY,
"THE TEACHER IS HERE AND
IS CALLING FOR YOU." AND
WHEN SHE HEARD IT, SHE ROSE
QUICKLY AND WENT TO HIM.

JOHN 11:28–29

LOOKING BEYOND YOURSELF

It was just one of those days when I found myself alone in the friary, taking care of everything by myself—cooking, cleaning, and doing it all. I couldn't help but grumble, wondering where all my fellow brothers were when I needed them. And just when I was trying to answer the ringing phone, the pot of beans on the stove started to burn. I felt so frustrated, trying to manage everything on my own.

And then the doorbell rang. I didn't know who it could be, but I was in no mood to deal with anyone else at that moment. I felt as if whoever was at the door was adding to my frustration. But when I opened the door, I saw a little girl standing there with her younger siblings. They looked down at the ground, and the girl looked up at me with her big, brown Honduran eyes and asked if I could teach her how to pray. She said that she had been told that the friars would be able to teach her. Still frustrated, I told her that the Poor Clares down the road might be more helpful. She said she had just come from there, and they said the friars would help her.

I felt trapped by God at that moment. I couldn't say no to this little girl's request. All of my frustration melted away, and I invited them in. I decided that I would teach them how to pray the Rosary. I went into the room and got a rosary, and we began to pray together. I also found out that the little girl wasn't going to school, because she had to help her mother sell food to make ends meet since her father had died in an accident.

This little girl taught me that responding to the Lord's call, even when it's difficult, is more important than prioritizing my own perceived emotional well-being. What was really more important in that moment? A pot of beans, or responding to children who are wondering how to find God in their struggles? God in his gentleness coaxed me to look beyond myself.

Mary does the same thing in this gospel. She was busy in the house dealing with arrangements surrounding her brother's death. She probably felt as if the whole world was crashing around her. Yet when she heard that Jesus was looking for her, she dropped it all and went to him.

Don't get me wrong, attending to our duties and self-care is essential, but it should never come at the expense of answering God's call. When we are feeling overwhelmed, let's take a step back and look at what's really important. With that vision, we'll come back to the practices that place us close to God's heart. With that relationship in place, everything else is negotiable.

REFLECT

1. Have you ever felt overwhelmed and then someone came to you in need? How did you respond? How might you ask Jesus to help you respond in such situations in the future?
2. Can you ask the Holy Spirit to help you be aware of and heed his promptings that may come during your day-to-day activities?
3. What prayer routine can you start this Lent and try to continue afterward so that you can nurture your heart to be alert to the Holy Spirit's call?

———————————————————————————————

———————————————————————————————

———————————————————————————————

———————————————————————————————

———————————————————————————————

_____

_____

_____

_____

_____

_____

PRAY

_I PRAY THIS DAY, LORD, FOR
THE AREAS OF MY LIFE THAT
ARE MISMANAGED OR OUT OF
CONTROL. I PRAY FOR THE AREAS
WITHIN MY HEART THAT ARE MESSY
AND UNKEMPT. LORD, I GIVE YOU
PERMISSION TO COME AND GENTLY
PUT THINGS IN BETTER ORDER. THE
CLOSER I GET TO YOU, THE MORE
MESS I FIND IN MY LIFE. PLEASE
TEACH ME TO PRAY. PLEASE SEE MY
POVERTY AND LIFT ME UP. I THANK
YOU, LORD, FOR YOU WILL NOT
LEAVE ME ABANDONED._

THEN JESUS, DEEPLY MOVED AGAIN, CAME TO THE TOMB; IT WAS A CAVE, AND A STONE LAY UPON IT. JESUS SAID, "TAKE AWAY THE STONE." MARTHA, THE SISTER OF THE DEAD MAN, SAID TO HIM, "LORD, BY THIS TIME THERE WILL BE AN ODOR, FOR HE HAS BEEN DEAD FOUR DAYS." JESUS SAID TO HER, "DID I NOT TELL YOU THAT IF YOU WOULD BELIEVE YOU WOULD SEE THE GLORY OF GOD?" SO THEY TOOK AWAY THE STONE.

JOHN 11:38–41A

POVERTY CHECK—
REMOVING THE STONE

As we reflect on the biblical story of Martha and Jesus, we can picture the scene where Jesus commands, "Take away the stone." Martha expresses her concern that the smell will be overwhelming, given that Lazarus has been dead for four days. Jesus reminds her to believe and assures her that they will witness God's glory. Without hesitation, Martha takes charge and directs people to remove the stone. Her determination and decisiveness serve as an example for us and invite us into a deeper sense of poverty.

In these challenging times of uncertainty, fear, and loss, we need to ask ourselves: "What stone is the Lord asking me to remove?" Sometimes, we bury things in our lives that need to be addressed. While confessing our past mistakes is crucial, and the forgiveness we receive in the sacrament is real, we might still want to offer something up to God. For instance, you might remember a past mistake and realize in a deeper way the damage it caused. Or you might be trying to change certain faults, but keep falling back into them. Such experiences may require us to examine our relationships with honesty and offer them to the Lord, trusting that he is at work in them.

We all make mistakes that act as stones that seal up our relationships with others and with God. Instead of focusing on petty issues, we should prioritize reconciling with others and making the most of our time. When we act decisively to remove these stones, we allow the Lord to work in our lives and bring new life to areas that need his holy touch. It might be uncomfortable or risky, but the Lord hears our prayers. Sometimes we need to act and participate in his work for him to do more for us. This kind of action requires us to be poor in spirit because we'd rather keep our sense of righteousness intact. Our practice of poverty can help us let go of that ego and to welcome the humility it takes to embrace the truth.

Let us be like Martha, who removed the stone without hesitation, and allow the Lord to work in our lives. We can trust that, if we believe, we will see the glory of God.

REFLECT

1. In what ways have you buried past experiences, and how are they impacting your life today?
2. How does being humble and poor in spirit allow you to be more open to God's healing action in your life?
3. Is there someone you need to reconcile with, or do you feel called to make up in some way for a mistake you made in the past? How can you do so this Lent?

_____

_____

_____

_____

_____

_____

PRAY

*LORD, WHAT IS THE STONE THAT YOU
ARE ASKING TO REMOVE IN MY LIFE?
WHAT AREA HAVE I BEEN HIDING,
WHAT PAIN HAVE I BEEN FESTERING
WITHIN, WHAT SHAME HAVE I
COVERED? LORD, IN YOUR MERCY,
GRANT ME THE GRACE TO DESIRE FOR
THAT STONE TO BE MOVED. GRANT
ME THE GRACE TO BRING TO THE
LIGHT OF CONFESSION THAT WHICH
WAS ONCE IN DARKNESS. THROUGH
THE SACRAMENT, ALLOW THE PART OF
ME THAT WAS DEAD TO COME BACK
TO LIFE.*

FIFTH WEEK OF LENT

SATURDAY

THEN MARY, WHEN SHE CAME WHERE
JESUS WAS AND SAW HIM, FELL AT HIS
FEET, SAYING TO HIM, "LORD, IF YOU
HAD BEEN HERE, MY BROTHER WOULD
NOT HAVE DIED." WHEN JESUS SAW
HER WEEPING, AND THE JEWS WHO
CAME WITH HER ALSO WEEPING, HE
WAS DEEPLY MOVED IN SPIRIT AND
TROUBLED; AND HE SAID, "WHERE
HAVE YOU LAID HIM?" THEY SAID TO
HIM, "LORD, COME AND SEE." JESUS
WEPT. SO THE JEWS SAID, "SEE HOW
HE LOVED HIM!" BUT SOME OF THEM
SAID, "COULD NOT HE WHO OPENED
THE EYES OF THE BLIND MAN HAVE
KEPT THIS MAN FROM DYING?"

JOHN 11:32–37

WEEPING WITH OTHERS

What is the shortest verse in the Bible? It's found in John chapter 11, verse 35, where it says, "Jesus wept." These two words may be short, but they carry great significance. It's surprising that Jesus, knowing that he would raise Lazarus from the dead, still wept with Mary and those who were mourning. This act shows us that God enters into our suffering and feels with us. It is a revelation of authentic empathy, which involves truly listening to and sharing with someone. Empathy means to "suffer with" somebody. Jesus's response here shows us that it's essential to walk with others in their good and bad times.

Sometimes, though, we brush off others' suffering, telling them to "suck it up" or "snap out of it." Perhaps we need to process our own emotions before we can be fully present and faithful to the person before us. Showing up for people when they are hurting means more than we know—they remember who stood by them in their bad times more than those who were there in their good times.

I spoke to a nurse who was taking some time off after the pandemic. Her profession is in high demand, and she could have "powered through"; however, she wisely took time to go on pilgrimage to deepen her relationship with God. She had seen so many difficult things these past years and needed time for renewal—for her heart to love freely. I listened to her story and encouraged her to take the time she needed. Her gratitude was reflected by the relieved smile on her face.

Jesus needed to weep with Mary and those who were suffering. Why? Not because God needed to weep, but because we needed him to be with us in those moments. He's with us in our moments of suffering and grief. Don't doubt it. He'll be with us always, with the plan of raising us from the dead.

REFLECT

1. How does it comfort you to know that even Jesus wept when his friend had died?
2. Do you regularly take time out from the busyness of life to recharge through prayer? If not, can you strive to do so starting this Lent?
3. Is there someone you know who is suffering through grief or loss? In what way do you feel called to accompany them as Jesus accompanied his friends in their grief?

PRAY

LORD, YOU WERE THERE. YOU WERE THERE WEEPING WITH ME. IN THAT TIME OF LOSS, WHEN MY LOVED ONE DIED, YOU WERE THERE. IN THAT HEARTBREAK, IN THE ISOLATION, WHEN I FELT COMPLETELY ALONE, LORD JESUS, YOU WERE WEEPING WITH ME. THANK YOU, LORD, FOR ALLOWING ME TO MOURN. THANK YOU, LORD, FOR NOT TELLING ME TO JUST MOVE ON. YOU ALLOW ME THE SPACE I NEED AND THEN BRING ME BACK TO LIFE. THANK YOU, LORD.

HOLY WEEK

WALKING IN HOLINESS

HOLY WEEK
PALM SUNDAY

WHEN THE DAYS DREW NEAR FOR
HIM TO BE RECEIVED UP, HE SET
HIS FACE TO GO TO JERUSALEM.

LUKE 9:51

ENTERING JERUSALEM

As Jesus rode into Jerusalem on a donkey, the crowds welcomed him with palm branches and shouts of "Hosanna!" Little did they know that he was beginning the culminating phase of his mission to save all of us. By entering into Jerusalem, Jesus was willingly walking the path that would ultimately lead to his death on the Cross.

Through his sacrifice, he redeemed us and instituted the sacraments for our sanctification. So this week, let's focus on the final steps on our journey to the Cross, tomb, and Resurrection, as well as on the sacraments that the Church gives us to join Jesus on the way to the Father.

"The sacraments are efficacious signs of grace" (*CCC* 1131), which means they are more than just signs or symbols. They do point us to God in the way a symbol does, but they also make God's presence real—they communicate grace to us. The Holy Spirit is at work in us through sacraments; they make us holy. It's not a stretch to say that the sacraments divinize us—they make us like God in that they give us a share in God's life.

We also have a sacramental view of all reality. Grace comes to us through the seven sacraments, yes, but every part of creation points us to our Creator. It doesn't take much imagination to see this truth: if you have been kissed by your grandmother, or marveled at a sunset, or laughed with friends over a home-cooked meal, you've seen how creation puts us in touch with God. This is a Catholic way to see the world that comes from a sacramental imagination.

So let us take this Palm Sunday as an opportunity to reflect on the deeper significance of this day and how it shapes our lives as Catholics—to contemplate the sacramental life and how God shares his life with us. Here at the threshold of Holy Week, we ponder the great act of love that Jesus offered in giving his life for us so that we can share in his Resurrection. Perhaps your observance of Lent this year has been perfect, or perhaps it has been hit-and-miss. No matter—today, we set our faces to go up to Jerusalem with our Lord, where we will follow him to the Cross with the hope that God can make us new.

REFLECT

1. Do you value the sacraments as efficacious signs of grace, gifts from God for our sanctification? How can you better make use of the sacraments in your life?

2. Do you see the world sacramentally? What are some ways that you have noticed God's presence through nature, meals with friends, love of family, and so on?

3. What commitment can you make today to participate in a special way in the Church's liturgy this Holy Week in order to accompany Jesus on his journey to the Cross?

PRAY

LORD, MY CRY OF "HOSANNA" WITH
THE CROWD IS A SHOUT FROM
DEEP WITHIN ME THAT GOD MAY BE
GOD IN MY LIFE. I GROW TIRED OF
MY MEDIOCRITY; I AM WORN OUT
BY HALF-HEARTEDNESS. YET, MY
RESPONSE IS THE SAME AS ALWAYS—I
TRY TO BRING CHANGE. YET THE
WHOLE TIME IT IS YOU WHO WILL
ENTER INTO THE JERUSALEM OF
MY EXISTENCE—TO BE WELCOMED,
TO BE LOVED, TO BE MOCKED, TO
BE REJECTED—ALL WITHIN ME. SO
AGAIN I CRY, "HOSANNA!" HELP
ME, LORD.

MONDAY

IS ANYONE AMONG YOU SICK?
LET HIM CALL FOR THE ELDERS
OF THE CHURCH, AND LET THEM
PRAY OVER HIM, ANOINTING HIM
WITH OIL IN THE NAME OF THE
LORD.

JAMES 5:14

FAITH HANDED ON

In many dioceses today, the bishop and priests gather to celebrate the Chrism Mass and pray an ancient rite that blesses the oils used for the sacraments. At this Mass, priests also renew their promises of celibacy and obedience. It's a Mass that calls special attention to the lineage of faith that has been handed on to us.

As the dozens of priests stream toward the sanctuary at the Chrism Mass, we recall how Jesus and his disciples gathered at the Last Supper, where he gave us his Body and Blood. After Jesus's Ascension, the early Christian community continued to gather to break bread and share the Word. As those communities grew, the disciples formed leaders to take their place. They laid hands on these leaders, who became bishops who later laid hands on priests to share their work. Down through the ages, we can trace our faith back to Christ and the disciples through physical touch. In fact, if you've received the Sacrament of Confirmation, it's no stretch to imagine Christ himself reaching out to touch you through the ages: He laid hands on the disciples, who laid hands on bishops, who laid hands on other bishops as they were ordained. Over the generations, those hands came to rest on your head to spread that heavenly fragranced chrism oil and anoint you with the Holy Spirit.

That chrism has its origin here at this Mass, where it is consecrated every year along with the other oils used for sacraments: the oil of the sick and the oil of catechumens that is used to prepare for Baptism. Chrism oil is used at Baptism, Confirmation, and Ordination—anytime a sacrament fundamentally changes who we are—so of the three oils, it is pretty special. That's why it smells so good—it's mixed with balsam. When the bishop and priests bless it, the bishop stirs in the perfume and literally blows into the container to signify the action of the Holy Spirit.

Why do we use oil in the first place? In the ancient world, oil was used for healing, protection, and strengthening. Athletes covered their bodies in oil to help them perform well. This is the Catholic way: to use natural signs like oil in our prayer as a means to make God's healing, protection, and strength real through grace.

As we pray through Holy Week, we give thanks for the faith that has been handed down to us in physical ways, as well as for those who made God's grace real for us through their loving touch. May our journey to the Cross and into Easter shape us into people who make faith, hope, and love real for others.

REFLECT

1. What do you think of the tradition of blessing chrism oil, of the ancient significance of oil for strength and healing, and of the breath symbolizing the Holy Spirit? How do these ideas influence your appreciation of this sacramental and the sacraments in which it is used?
2. Have you considered before the continuous succession of the apostles through the laying on of hands by bishops all the way through to those priests and bishops you know today? How does this help you value the Church's tradition and the priesthood?
3. How might you pray in a special way today for the priests and bishops who have influenced your life, passing on to you the faith that they received from those before them?

PRAY

*YOUR GRACE IS ENOUGH, LORD.
YOUR GRACE THAT YOU POUR DOWN
UPON ME IS ENOUGH. THE GRACE
THAT FLOWS FROM THE SACRAMENTS
YOU GAVE TO ME WITH SUCH LOVING
CONCERN IS ENOUGH. YET, I ASK,
LORD, FOR MORE AT THIS TIME.
CALLING ON THE GRACE OF THE
SACRAMENTS I HAVE RECEIVED, I ASK
YOU TO DEEPEN MY UNDERSTANDING
OF THEIR SIGNIFICANCE.*

HOLY WEEK

TUESDAY

WE KNOW THAT THE WHOLE
CREATION HAS BEEN GROANING
WITH LABOR PAINS TOGETHER
UNTIL NOW; AND NOT ONLY THE
CREATION, BUT WE OURSELVES,
WHO HAVE THE FIRST FRUITS OF
THE SPIRIT, GROAN INWARDLY
AS WE WAIT FOR ADOPTION AS
SONS, THE REDEMPTION OF
OUR BODIES.

ROMANS 8:22–23

SEEKING FORGIVENESS

Pope Francis has spoken of how the greatest evil of our day is the loss of our sense of sin. But we know that this condition is not new; it has been true since Adam and Eve! As we meditate on the events leading up to the Passion and Death of Christ, we must recognize our own brokenness and struggle to do good while resisting evil. This has been the whole point of our Lenten journey and our focus on poverty: to surface for ourselves the ways in which we are blind to our own selfishness. This is a good time to gather up the insights we've gained along the way and take an honest look at ourselves before we enter the Paschal Mystery at the end of the week.

A good practice here would be to review the notes you've written for yourself throughout this journal. Do any habits or patterns appear? Are there recurring relationships or situations that you see in a new light? What are the consistent challenges you've faced in your Lenten journey? What aspects of poverty have been a struggle? Your insights will be mixed with light and darkness. Take some time to give thanks for the grace God has given you to sustain you thus far. Also take some time to face the truth of your brokenness.

In the midst of our darkness, we are reminded of the hope that we have in Jesus Christ. Through his life, death, and Resurrection, he has opened the way for us to be restored to a right relationship with God. The Sacrament of Confession is a great gift that restores us to right relationship with God. In the confessional, we meet Christ through the words of the priest (see *CCC* 1548). I encourage you to try to go to Confession today or tomorrow, as part of your preparation for Easter.

Let us remember that we are part of the family of God, members of the Body of Christ that is the Church. Our struggles with sin are not unique, yet through the grace of God, we have the opportunity to become temples of the Holy Spirit. May we use these final days of Lent to deepen our relationship with God and to become more like Christ in all that we do.

REFLECT

1. Looking back at your time with this journal, what patterns appear? What do you feel Jesus is challenging you to change in your life in order to follow him more closely?
2. In what ways would you like to thank Jesus for graces you have received so far through your prayer with this journal?
3. Can you make a commitment to go to Confession today or tomorrow to prepare for the Triduum?

PRAY

*JESUS, BLESS THE MINISTER WHO
PUT THE OIL ON MY FOREHEAD AT
THE MOMENT OF MY BAPTISM. BLESS
THE HANDS THAT HELPED ME AND
NURTURED ME IN THE FAITH. BLESS
THE LIGHT THAT CAME FROM THE
CANDLE SYMBOLIZING THE LIGHT
THAT SHONE IN ME. ANOINT ME
ANEW WITH A FRESH OUTPOURING
OF GRACE, THAT I MAY BECOME THE
FRAGRANT OFFERING YOU DESIRE
OF ME.*

BUT JESUS SAID TO HIM, "JUDAS,
WOULD YOU BETRAY THE SON
OF MAN WITH A KISS?"

LUKE 22:48

VISION

Today is popularly called Spy Wednesday. Why? It's the day we read Matthew 26, which recounts how Judas Iscariot went to the Sanhedrin and asked how much they would give him if he turned Jesus over to them. For thirty pieces of silver, Judas eventually betrayed Jesus.

Let's look in scripture for a passage where another just man was sold for pieces of silver. Joseph in Genesis had eleven brothers, and he was his father's favorite son. Jacob loved Joseph and gave him a special coat (maybe you saw the musical *Joseph and the Amazing Technicolor Dreamcoat*). Joseph's brothers became jealous of this special attention and did away with him; they sold him to slavery, and he ended up in Egypt. Because he had vision, he rose through the ranks of slaves to even advise the pharaoh himself. When a drought threatened the region and his own family came begging for food, Joseph was in a position to help.

It's an amazing story, one that could have ended early if Joseph had given in to despair when his brothers betrayed him. That must have felt like the end of his life, but it was just the beginning of a journey by which he would become a blessing to the known world.

Judas did not have that same kind of hope. He betrayed Jesus and then took his own life because he could not see through the darkness he was in. Jesus reconciled with all of the disciples who deserted him when he was arrested. We can wonder how he would have reconciled with Judas as well if Judas had remained open to that possibility. The Resurrection proves that God has power to draw good out of the worst of situations.

Here in the middle of Holy Week, let us adopt a "paschal vision"—let us never stop looking for the good that God can do. Judas's betrayal was the beginning of the worst thing that could happen: the murder of God's own Son. Yet, like Joseph, we've been given hope to see that even betrayal is not betrayal—it is the beginning of victory. Let victory reign in us.

REFLECT

1. How does Jesus's offer of mercy to all who betrayed him make you feel? Have you considered that Judas would have been offered mercy if he had gone to Jesus in repentance? What can you learn from this?

2. In what ways does the story of Joseph in the Old Testament give you hope that God can work through even the worst situations?

3. How can you adopt a "paschal vision" in order to keep looking for the good God can do, even in difficult and seemingly hopeless situations?

_____

_____

_____

_____

_____

_____

_____

_____

_____

PRAY

_GRANT ME, LORD, THE GRACE TO
FORGIVE THOSE WHO HAVE WOUNDED
AND BETRAYED ME, THOSE WHO
TRIED TO BRING ME DOWN. I BLESS
THEM, LORD. LET A BLESSING COME
UPON THEM EVEN IF THE PAIN IS
STILL EXTANT, EVEN IF THE WOUND
IS STILL FRESH. I FORGIVE THEM,
LORD, SO MY TRESPASSES MAY BE
FORGIVEN._

HOLY THURSDAY

MY FATHER, IF IT BE POSSIBLE,
LET THIS CHALICE PASS FROM
ME; NEVERTHELESS, NOT AS I
WILL, BUT AS YOU WILL.

MATTHEW 26:39

THE LAST SUPPER

Holy Thursday technically marks the end of our Lenten journey because we've arrived at the moment we've been waiting for: the Triduum! That's a word that describes the three days in which we walk through the Passion, Death, and Resurrection of Jesus. The Triduum begins with Holy Thursday Mass this evening and does not end until the Easter Vigil on Saturday night.

When I say it does not end, that's very literal. We remember the Last Supper tonight at Holy Thursday Mass, which ends with a procession with the Eucharist. If you pay attention, you'll notice that there's no final blessing: after Communion, the priests carry the Eucharist and place it in a tabernacle of repose for prayer. We are invited to join the disciples who waited for the Lord as he prayed in the Garden of Gethsemane, knowing that he would die the next day.

The rest of the services during the Triduum are considered one continuous prayer of worship. The services tomorrow on Good Friday begin without a greeting and end without a closing. The Easter Vigil begins with the lighting of the paschal fire, but there's no normal greeting. We're outside of time now; starting with Holy Thursday Mass, we've entered the Paschal Mystery. We come together at various points to connect in prayer, but essentially, we are walking through the next three days with Jesus as he carries his Cross, is placed in the tomb, and is resurrected with the dawn of Easter breaking on our lives.

The power of our shared prayer as Catholics is on full display in the Triduum. Jesus gathered with his disciples two thousand years ago for his Last Supper, but he is the Lord of time and space. When we gather tonight, we sit at that table as well. In fact, we gather at that same table every time we go to Mass. The things that happen at the Last Supper, on Calvary, and in the tomb are not confined to history. We don't just remember those moments—we *live* them.

For forty days, we've been moving toward these final steps to Calvary and through the empty tomb, making ourselves ready to walk with Christ. Let us step forward today with courage, knowing that by following Christ, we gain his strength to carry the crosses that appear in our daily lives and receive the new life that God promises us.

REFLECT

1. How can you spend time with Jesus in prayer this evening of Holy Thursday, joining him in Gethsemane as he prepares for his Passion and Death?

2. Did you know that we participate in the Last Supper at each Mass? How does this idea give you a deeper understanding of the Sacrament of the Eucharist?

3. How can you pray today to step forward with Jesus in courage toward the Cross so that you can join in the Resurrection?

_____

_____

_____

_____

_____

_____

PRAY

*THANK YOU, LORD, FOR YOUR
BODY AND BLOOD GIVEN UP FOR
ME. THANK YOU FOR THE GIFT OF
THE HOLY EUCHARIST. THANK YOU
FOR THE GIFT OF EUCHARISTIC
ADORATION. TRANSFORM ME INTO
YOU, LORD, AND I RECEIVE YOU INTO
ME. MAY WHAT IS HOLY TRANSFORM
THAT WHICH IS UNHOLY. MAY WHAT
IS GIVEN FOR THE SAKE OF LIFE
HEAL THAT WHICH IS DESERVING OF
DEATH. MAY MY BODY ALSO BE GIVEN
UP FOR YOU. AMEN.*

HE WAS WOUNDED FOR
OUR TRANSGRESSIONS,
HE WAS BRUISED FOR OUR
INIQUITIES; UPON HIM WAS
THE CHASTISEMENT THAT
MADE US WHOLE, AND WITH
HIS STRIPES WE ARE HEALED.

ISAIAH 53:5

HOPEFUL MOURNING

Good Friday is a day of reflection. I hope you can have some silence this morning when we remember the sacrifice of Jesus Christ. At noon, parishes around the world will pray the Stations of the Cross. As followers of Christ, we believe that he is the chosen Messiah of God, who was promised to us. He was born as a baby in Bethlehem and taught among us. He was crucified on the Cross to conquer sin, but he rose gloriously from the dead, appearing to his disciples. Through his Ascension, he was exalted at the right hand of the Father and now summons all to him through the ministry of the Church.

His saving work requires a response from us to repent of our sins and live in the new life that Christ offers. This alone will prepare us for the coming judgment that is to come at the end of time. We should have some urgency to conform our lives to Christ—we don't have unlimited time to get right with God!

Although Good Friday recalls the most unjust act in history, it was also an amazing victory. Jesus took the cross, which before was a sign of condemnation, and turned it into the sign of our victory. Jesus went to the Cross to save us from eternal death. We are saved through his blood shed on the Cross.

Our scripture from Isaiah captures what was promised. Through his wounds, we are healed. He paid the price that we could not pay. Our debt is paid, and we are forgiven through the blood of the Lamb. Sacramentally, we experience the healing forgiveness of sins through two sacraments: Confession and Anointing of the Sick.

Good Friday is a day when we should be still and reflect on what Jesus did for us. He took our sins upon himself and died on the Cross to save us from eternal death. This is why we call it *Good* Friday. It is a day of mourning and sadness, but it is also a day of hope because of what Jesus has done for us. We need to take the time to repent and turn our hearts toward Christ. Through him, we can find healing, forgiveness, and hope for the future.

REFLECT

1. How do you plan to take time out today for silence and reflection on the Passion and Death of Jesus?
2. In what ways do you celebrate Good Friday as both a day of mourning and a day of hope?
3. How is Good Friday a reminder to prepare for our own death and judgment, in prayer, repentance, and hope?

PRAY

HEAVENLY FATHER, I REVERENCE THE WOUNDS PRINTED ONTO YOUR SON'S INNOCENT HANDS. I WEEP, FOR THE CONDEMNATION WAS MINE, YET HE PAID THE PRICE FOR ME. MAY HIS ASCENT UP CALVARY HILL STRENGTHEN ME TO DESCEND DOWN MY MOUNTAIN OF PRIDE. MAY HIS WORDS OF FORGIVENESS SAID WITH ARMS OUTSTRETCHED HELP ME TO OPEN MY HAND TO FORGIVE AND HELP MY NEIGHBOR. MAY HIS PIERCED SIDE BECOME A FOUNTAIN OF TRANSFORMATIVE LOVE THAT TURNS MY SADNESS, ANGER, AND ANXIETY INTO A SIMPLE JOY AT BEING FORGIVEN.

HOLY WEEK

HOLY SATURDAY

IN SAYING, "HE ASCENDED,"
WHAT DOES IT MEAN BUT THAT
HE HAD ALSO DESCENDED
INTO THE LOWER PARTS OF THE
EARTH? HE WHO DESCENDED IS
HE WHO ALSO ASCENDED FAR
ABOVE ALL THE HEAVENS, THAT
HE MIGHT FILL ALL THINGS.

EPHESIANS 4:9–10

HOLY WAITING

As we meditate on this Saturday of Holy Week, let us ponder Jesus buried in the tomb and the silence and stillness surrounding us. The earth itself feels hushed, for our King is asleep. Today, we recall how God took on human flesh, descended into the realm of the dead, and shook hell's foundations with his presence. We profess in the Apostles' Creed: "He descended into hell." He descended so he could ascend.

Today, we contemplate Christ's loving pursuit of all those who died in darkness and sorrow. With the Cross as his triumphant weapon, Christ approaches those in despair, offering salvation not just to them, but to all humanity. Paul translates this action as we experience it in our own lives when we are awakened by his grace: "Awake, O sleeper, and arise from the dead, and Christ shall give you light" (Ephesians 5:14).

With Jesus as our divine shepherd and liberator, let us gratefully accept his invitation to rise from our slumber and be freed from any bondage that enslaves us. Remembering that we are created in his image, and he resides within each one of us, let us walk toward eternal life together with him.

As we reflect on the Lamb that was slain to give us life and deliverance from death, may our hearts overflow with gratitude for the sacrifice made by Jesus Christ. Contemplate how he came down from heaven and took on our humanity so we could be healed in body and soul.

As a testament to his love, he bore our suffering in his vulnerable human body that was led forth like a lamb to be slaughtered like a sheep. In doing so, he ransomed and freed us from our earthly bondage and sealed our souls with His Spirit.

Embrace this Passover mystery, because your salvation lies at the heart of it. On that solemn day, he was taken and crucified upon the tree. Yet his body did not decay in the tomb, and on this Saturday of Holy Week, we eagerly await his miraculous Resurrection that will bring life and light to all. May we be filled with gratitude for our deliverance from death and anticipate the coming celebration of Christ's Resurrection.

REFLECT

1. In what ways can you meditate today on Jesus as the Lamb of God who gave up his body in death in order to save you?
2. What inspires you about Jesus's time in the tomb when his body did not decay but awaited the Resurrection? How does this give you hope for the sacredness God bestows on your own body and for his promise of resurrection of the dead?
3. Can you make a commitment to visit the grave of a loved one soon and to pray for their soul, that they may be resurrected with Jesus?

PRAY

*IN THE SILENCE, LORD, YOU SPEAK.
IN THE SILENCE OF THIS DAY, A
WORD IS RISING UP FROM THE
DEPTHS. LORD, HELP ME LOOK AT
MY LIFE AND SINCERELY CHANGE.
ALL IS FROM YOUR GRACE, BUT
STRENGTHEN MY WILL TO BE ABOUT
YOUR BUSINESS, LORD. MOVE ME
TO BELIEVE MORE DEEPLY IN YOUR
SALVIFIC LOVE FOR ME. I AWAIT YOU
IN THE SILENCE.*

EASTER SUNDAY

BUT MARY STOOD WEEPING OUTSIDE
THE TOMB, AND AS SHE WEPT SHE
STOOPED TO LOOK INTO THE TOMB;
AND SHE SAW TWO ANGELS IN WHITE,
SITTING WHERE THE BODY OF JESUS
HAD LAIN, ONE AT THE HEAD AND
ONE AT THE FEET. THEY SAID TO HER,
"WOMAN, WHY ARE YOU WEEPING?"
SHE SAID TO THEM, "BECAUSE THEY
HAVE TAKEN AWAY MY LORD, AND I DO
NOT KNOW WHERE THEY HAVE LAID
HIM." . . . JESUS SAID TO HER, "MARY."
SHE TURNED AND SAID TO HIM IN
HEBREW, "RAB-BO'NI!" (WHICH MEANS
TEACHER).

JOHN 20:11–13, 16

OPEN YOURSELF
TO GOD'S MESSAGE

I invite you to take a few deep breaths. As you inhale, fill your lungs with the hope and joy that Easter Sunday brings. His love is our life! Breathe in life! You are redeemable! Jesus makes it so. As you exhale, let go of any burden, doubt, or tension. What incredible joy! What a deep, unfathomable joy! Death is destroyed. Jesus is alive.

Let us walk with one of the people who was there on that fateful morning. Let us focus our meditation on the remarkable story of Mary Magdalene, who played an extraordinary role in the Resurrection narrative. Her journey teaches us valuable lessons about faith, persistence, and personal transformation.

Put yourself in Mary's situation. Imagine you're walking along the path to Jesus's tomb early in the morning. Feel her determination and devotion as she sets out toward an uncertain destination.

Mary Magdalene had once been lost to sin but found her true purpose in Jesus's words and compassion. Like her, allow yourself to be open to the transformative power of Christ. Embrace your own imperfections, and do not let them squelch your joy. Mary Magdalene did not quite understand what was happening when she first met the risen Lord, yet she still was the first to announce the Resurrection. It gives me great hope to recognize that even those who have made mistakes can spread the Good News and be instruments of God's sweet song of salvation.

Visualize yourself standing near the empty tomb alongside Mary Magdalene. Can you feel her sorrow when she searches for Jesus's body? Do you sense her desire to hold on to her pain? Let this moment remind you that it is possible—even necessary—for each of us to release our pain and suffering in order to be fully open to God's message.

Now imagine her surprise and joy when she discovers that Jesus is alive. See her face transform when she recognizes him, and hear her share the incredible news that he is risen!

Has it ever happened that you went from sadness to joy? It is like the best Confession you ever had: incredible relief and joy, gratitude and disbelief, all at once.

Strengthen your faith today by recognizing the incredible ways God works through each one of us, regardless of past mistakes or imperfections. Breathe in deeply the promise of resurrection and the knowledge that Jesus is always with us. Let us be renewed and inspired to share the Good News with those around us, just as Mary Magdalene did.

Happy Easter!

REFLECT

1. How does it give you hope that Mary Magdalene, who was once a great sinner, was the first to announce the Resurrection?
2. When have you experienced sadness turn into joy? Have you experienced this spiritually through the sacraments? How does this experience strengthen your faith?
3. How do you feel renewed on this Easter Sunday, after your Lenten journey of prayer?

PRAY

*CHRIST IS RISEN. LET HIM BE
GLORIFIED IN MY LIFE, IN MY
FAMILY, AND IN MY WORLD. LET HIM
BE GLORIFIED IN MY PAST, PRESENT,
AND FUTURE. LET HIM BE GLORIFIED
IN MY WEAKNESS, IN MY GIFTEDNESS,
AND IN MY POWERLESSNESS. CHRIST,
RISE AGAIN IN ME.*

FR. AGUSTINO TORRES, CFR, is a priest with the Franciscan Friars of the Renewal, where he serves on the community's council. He is the founder of Corazón Puro. He is the author of *Prepare Your Heart* and serves as a retreat guide, spiritual director, and an international youth and young adult speaker.

Torres hosts the EWTN TV shows *ICONS* and *Clic con Corazón Puro* (in both English and Spanish) and the National Eucharistic Revival podcast *Revive*.

https://www.corazonpuro.org/
Facebook: The Community of the Franciscan Friars of the Renewal
Instagram: @oralecp
YouTube: @CorazonPuroNyc

VALERIE DELGADO is a Catholic painter, a digital artist, and the owner of Pax.Beloved. She illustrated the books *Prepare Your Heart* by Fr. Agustino Torres, CFR, *Adore* by Fr. John Burns, *Restore* by Sr. Miriam James Heidland, SOLT, and *ABC Get to Know the Saints with Me* by Caroline Perkins.

She lives in the Houston, Texas, area.

www.paxbeloved.com
Instagram: @pax.valerie

FREE *MADE FOR HEAVEN* COMPANION RESOURCES AND VIDEOS

Enhance your Lenten experience with these **FREE** resources. Perfect for individuals, parishes, small groups, and classrooms, they include:

- weekly companion videos with Fr. Agustino Torres, CFR
- *Made for Heaven Leader's Guide*
- pulpit and bulletin announcements
- downloadable flyers, posters, and digital graphics
- and more!

Scan here to access the free resources and videos or visit **avemariapress.com/private/page/made-for-heaven-resources**.